Geoffrey Chaucer

The Canterbury Tales

Text adaptation and activities by **Derek Sellen**

Additional activities by **Rebecca Raynes** and **Robert Hill**

Illustrated by **Giovanni Manna**

Editors: Rebecca Raynes, Robert Hill
Design and art direction: Nadia Maestri
Computer graphics: Simona Corniola
Picture research: Laura Lagomarsino

© 2007   Black Cat Publishing,
          an imprint of Cideb Editrice, Genoa, Canterbury

Picture Credits

By courtesy of the National Portrait Gallery, London: 5; The
Master and Fellows of Corpus Christi College, Cambridge: 7;
Bodleian Library (Douce 313 f. 394 v.), Oxford: 10; British
Library, London: 41; Christie's Colour Library: 105;
Österreichische Nationalbibliothek (Cod 2617, f. 53), Wien:
107

We would be happy to receive your comments and
suggestions, and give you any other information concerning
our material.
Our e-mail and web site addresses are:

www.blackcat-cideb.com

CISQ CISQ CERT
TEXTBOOKS AND
TEACHING MATERIALS
The quality of the publisher's
design, production and sales processes has
been certified to the standard of
UNI EN ISO 9001

ISBN 978-88-530-0638-7   Book + CD

Printed in Italy by Litoprint, Genoa

Contents

These stories are recorded in full.
These symbols indicate the beginning and end of the passages
linked to the listening activities.

Geoffrey Chaucer by an unknown artist.

Geoffrey Chaucer

Geoffrey Chaucer is often called 'the Father of English poetry', the first great writer in English. He was born in London in about 1340, the son of John Chaucer, an important wine merchant. [1] For most of his life, Geoffrey was connected with the royal court in London in various ways, and official records often mention his name.

When he was about sixteen, he became a servant in the household of one of the king's daughters-in-law. In 1359, he served as a soldier in the war in France. He was taken prisoner but released for a ransom, [2] part of which the king himself paid. During the 1360s, he worked in the King's household and was in contact with the sophisticated

1. **wine merchant** : a person who buys and sells wine.
2. **ransom** : money which is paid for the freedom of a prisoner.

society of the court. He married Philippa, a lady-in-waiting [1] to the Queen, and had at least two sons. One, Thomas Chaucer, went on to become one of the richest men in England. Geoffrey became closely connected to the powerful family of the Duke of Lancaster and wrote a famous poem on the death of the Duchess.

Chaucer describes himself in his writing as a fat man with a modest, simple personality. It seems that he was interested in religion but also enjoyed earthy [2] humour. Many of his works are about love and marriage, especially about the equality of men and women. At the end of *The Canterbury Tales*, he apologises for writing some stories which might seem anti-religious.

One of the most important events of his life was his visit to Italy in 1372. He stayed there for eleven months, visiting Genoa, Pisa and Florence. He already knew French literature very well, but now he came into contact with the works of Dante, Boccaccio and Petrarch. This Italian influence was very strong in his later work. The plan of *The Canterbury Tales* – where pilgrims tell stories to the others – is almost certainly based upon Boccaccio's *Decameron*, a collection of a hundred stories told by ten young people from Florence who escape the 'Black Death' or 'Plague' [3] in Florence and spend ten days in villas outside the town.

He also realised the importance of creating literature in the vernacular. [4] Dante had established Italian as a language to write poetry in; Chaucer wanted to do the same for English.

1. **lady-in-waiting** : companion.
2. **earthy** [ɜːθi] : basic, low, unsophisticated.
3. **the 'Plague'** : a disease that came to Europe from the East in 1347. It lasted till about 1350 and killed perhaps 25 million people, about a third of the population of Europe.
4. **the vernacular** : the common language of the people, not a literary form of language.

He had various important positions at court in the 1370s and 80s. We know that he went on a secret mission to France and visited Italy again. He had already completed some major works of literature and probably began *The Canterbury Tales* in about 1387. He never completed it. It was a huge project which would have included 120 stories if it had been finished: Chaucer intended that each pilgrim told two stories on the way to Canterbury and two on the way back, but he only wrote twenty-four.

At the time of writing *The Canterbury Tales,* he began to be short of money [1] but was able to live in a house in the garden of Westminster Abbey from 1399. He died in 1400 on 25 October at the age of about sixty and was buried in Westminster Abbey. This fact shows that he was popular with the king and the court. In the centuries since he died, other famous writers have been buried in the same area of the Abbey, which has become known as Poets' Corner.

1 Comprehension check

Answer the following questions. Try to answer from memory; look back at the text only if you really need to.

1 What is Geoffrey Chaucer often called?
2 When did his connection with the royal court begin?
3 How does Chaucer describe himself?
4 What are many of his works about?
5 What works did he come into contact with when he was in Italy?
6 What was his ambition for the English language?
7 How much of his original project for *The Canterbury Tales* did he complete?

1. **short of money** : without enough money.

6

The frontispiece of an early copy of Chaucer's **Troilus and Criseyde**, a poem about the unhappy story of two lovers during the Trojan war, written while Chaucer was beginning **The Canterbury Tales**. Chaucer (standing) is reading to the court of Richard II.

The towers of **Westminster Abbey**. The first building was finished in 1065, but the present building was begun in 1265. All English kings and queens except two have been crowned here. A short walk away are the Houses of Parliament.

 INTERNET PROJECT

Connect to the Internet and go to www.blackcat-cideb.com or www.cideb.it. Insert the title or part of the title of the book into our search engine. Open the page for *The Canterbury Tales*. Click on the Internet project link. Go down the page until you find the title of this book and click on the relevant link for this project.

▶ Who was the first writer buried in Poets' Corner, and why?

▶ What is unusual about the memorials of Shakespeare, Lord Byron and Charles Dickens?

▶ What is unusual about Thomas Parr?

▶ Visit some other places in the virtual tour of Westminster Abbey. What do you find interesting?

Chaucer's World

Chaucer lived in dangerous times. There were three kings during his lifetime: Edward III, who became less popular as he grew older; Richard II, who was probably murdered; Henry IV, who forced Richard II to stop being king. There was a long war against France and disagreements between the English king and the Pope.

The battle of Crécy, 26 August 1346 (French manuscript, 15th century). During the **Hundred Years War** (1337-1453) England tried to rule France. All the battles were in France: the English won several, including Crécy, but lost the war.

It was also the time of the 'Black Death' or Plague. This terrible disease was brought to England in 1348 by ships from the continent, [1] which carried the infection. It spread rapidly, carried by black rats. Perhaps as much as a third of the population of England died. Whole villages were destroyed. Both rich and poor were affected – three Archbishops of Canterbury died from the Plague. 'God is deaf,' [2] wrote the religious poet William Langland (1332-1400).

Religion, however, continued to be a powerful force. Many people

Pilgrims arrive on foot at the **Church of the Holy Sepulchre** in **Jerusalem** (French manuscript, 1410-12). Jerusalem was not an easy pilgrimage destination, but it was popular: the Wife of Bath went there three times!

1. **continent** : mainland Europe (not the British Isles).
2. **deaf** : unable to hear.

believed that the Plague was God's punishment for human beings. They believed in Hell [1] and were afraid that if they did not follow religion, they would burn in everlasting fires. The Church itself contained some bad men. Chaucer describes the Pardoner and the Summoner, who used their jobs in the Church to become rich. The Prioress, with her fine clothes and her little dogs, is a comfort-loving lady who sees religion as an opportunity to obtain a high social position.

Pilgrimages [2] were very popular. The most famous pilgrimage in England itself was the journey to Canterbury. People believed that Thomas Becket, who had been murdered in Canterbury Cathedral, could help the sick and answer prayers. [3] The Wife of Bath, another of Chaucer's pilgrims, has even been as far as Jerusalem on a pilgrimage. Some people became pilgrims for real religious reasons, but for many people it was simply a moment for a spring holiday (as you will see from the beginning on page 15!).

1 Comprehension check
Answer the following questions.

1 What was the 'Black Death'?
2 How does Chaucer criticise some members of the Church?
3 Why were pilgrimages popular?

2 Discussion
Can you think of any events which people go to in order to enjoy themselves, even though they say they have a 'serious' reason for going?

---

1. **Hell** : where bad people go after they die; opposite of Heaven.
2. **Pilgrimages** : journeys with a religious purpose to a special place, e.g. Mecca, Jerusalem, Santiago de Compostela, Lourdes.
3. **prayers** : requests to God; what we ask for from God.

The Characters

The picture on pages 12-13 shows the pilgrims that you will read about in Part One, the Prologue. Four of them have already got their horses, and the others are on the way to the stables to get their horses. Then they will all ride to Canterbury together.

Here is a key to the picture:
1 Chaucer, 2 the Knight, 3 the Squire, 4 the Countryman, 5 the Nun, 6 the Prioress, 7 the Nun's Secretary, 8-9-10 the Nun's Priests, 11 the Monk, 12 the Friar, 13 the Merchant, 14 the Cleric, 15 the Franklin, 16 the Cook, 17 the Sea-Captain, 18 the Doctor, 19 the Wife of Bath, 20 the Miller, 21 the Parson, 22 the Summoner, 23 the Pardoner, 24 the Host

Before you read

1 Reading pictures
Look at the picture of the pilgrims on pages 12-13. In pairs or small groups:

- choose two of the pilgrims that you think Chaucer will present critically;
- choose two of the pilgrims that you think Chaucer will present in a positive way.

Compare your choices in class.

2 Look at the picture on page 17, where the pilgrims are at dinner in a pub. How many of them can you recognise and name?

PART ONE

The Prologue

n April, when the sweet showers [1] fall and feed the roots in the earth, the flowers begin to bloom. [2] The soft wind blows from the west and the young sun rises in the sky. The small birds sing in the green forests. Then people want to go on pilgrimages. From every part of England, they go to Canterbury to visit the tomb [3] of Thomas Becket, the martyr, [4] who helped the sick.

My name is Geoffrey Chaucer. People say that I am a poet but I am not really very important. I am just a story-teller. One day in spring, I was staying in London at The Tabard Inn. [5] At night, a great crowd of people arrived at the inn, ready to go on a

1. **showers** : light rain.
2. **bloom** : come into flower.
3. **tomb** : a structure, usually made of stone, where a dead person is buried.
4. **martyr** : someone who is killed because of their religious (or political) beliefs.
5. **The Tabard Inn** : the name of the pub south of the River Thames where Chaucer and the pilgrims stayed. (A 'tabard' was a soldier's jacket.)

pilgrimage to Canterbury. I soon made friends with them and promised to join them.

'You must get up early,' they told me. 'We are leaving when the sun rises.'

Before I begin my story, I will describe the pilgrims to you. There were twenty-nine. There were men and women, young and old, fat and thin, ugly and beautiful, poor men and lords, some who lived good lives, others who were bad. If you want to know about the world of human beings, then go on a pilgrimage!

First of all, there was a Knight. He was a brave man who had fought for chivalry, [1] truth and honour. He had taken part in wars in all parts of the world. He always fought bravely and he always killed his enemy. Although he was a famous man, he was modest, sincere and polite. He was a perfect gentleman.

The Knight rode a fine horse but his clothes still carried the marks of war. He was going on the pilgrimage to thank God for his victories.

The Knight's son, a fine young Squire, [2] rode with him. He was twenty years old, with curly [3] hair and a handsome face. He had fought well in war to win the love of his lady. He knew how to ride well, to write songs and poems, to draw [4] and to dance. The girls all loved him, that handsome young man.

There was a Countryman riding with him. He carried a bow and arrows, a sword and a hunting horn. His face was brown and

---

1. **chivalry** : protecting ladies, being honest and other noble behaviour.
2. **Squire** : a young man who served a knight.
3. **curly** : not straight
4. **draw** : make pictures.

his clothes were green. There were peacock [1] feathers on his arrows. He was a true man of the forest.

Then there was an elegant Prioress. [2] Her name was Madam Eglantine. She spoke fine French with an English accent and had very good manners. When she was eating, she was careful not to make a mess. What a fine, sensitive lady! If she saw a mouse which was caught in a trap, [3] she cried. She gave roast meat or milk or fine white bread to her little dogs and, if one died, she was sad for weeks.

She had grey eyes, small soft red lips and a wide forehead. Her clothes were fashionable. She wore a graceful cloak, a coral bracelet, some beads and a golden brooch marked with an 'A'. 'Amor vincit omnia' was written on it. That is Latin — 'Love conquers all'.

There was another Nun, a Secretary and three Priests. Also, there was a fat Monk, who wore rich clothes and loved hunting. His favourite food was roast swan. [4] Next to him, there was a merry Friar. This fat Friar loved pretty girls, silver and gold and singing. He knew all the inns in town and loved drinking better than praying.

These were all religious people. But they loved the world — a fashionable lady, a rich monk and a pleasure-loving friar!

All kinds of people rode on the pilgrimage. There was a rich Merchant with a long beard and rich clothes. He knew how to

1. **peacock** : a beautiful bird, famous for its tail with 'eyes'.
2. **Prioress** : a female religious leader, the head of a group of nuns. Nuns (women) and monks and friars (men) live in religious communities.
3. **trap** : a thing to catch animals, e.g. mice.
4. **swan** : a big white bird.

make money and rode a fat horse. But next to him, the Oxford Cleric [1] rode a thin horse. He preferred to have books by great philosophers next to his bed, not bags of money. A Franklin [2] with a white beard rode with them, a man who loved good food and wine.

After them, there was a Cook who knew how to cook delicious meals with herbs and spices. [3] Then there was a brown-faced Sea-Captain who looked like a pirate. He had fought battles at sea and made his prisoners walk the plank. [4] Then there was a Doctor who knew everything about the body. His patients paid him with gold. The plague had made him very rich indeed!

Look at the next pilgrim! She was a large red-faced woman from the city of Bath. She wore a huge hat and a long coat over her wide hips. [5] Her tights [6] were red and her shoes were new. Her face was as red as her clothes. How many husbands do you think she had been married to? Five! She had lived longer than them all. That is how she became rich enough to go on pilgrimages, to Jerusalem, to Spain, to France, to Rome… The Wife of Bath liked to laugh and talk about love, a subject in which she was an expert! What a woman!

Now, I will tell you about the Miller. [7] He was a great, fat, strong man with a red beard and huge muscles. On the end of his

1. **Cleric** : religious scholar.
2. **Franklin** : land-owner.
3. **herbs and spices** : natural substances to add flavour to food.
4. **plank** : a long piece of wood. Pirates made their enemies walk off the ship and fall into the sea.
5. **hips** : the widest part of the body.
6. **tights** : covering for the legs.
7. **Miller** : a man who has a mill where corn is made into flour.

large red nose, there was a large red hairy wart. [1] The Miller loved drinking and telling jokes. But he was an expert thief who stole corn from his customers. As the pilgrims rode out of town, the Miller played the bagpipes. [2] Everyone knew that we were coming!

A Parson was also travelling with us. He loved God and loved to help other people. He gave money to the poor, gave advice to people with problems and visited the sick, even when the weather was bad. He was a very good man.

But behind him, I am sorry to tell you, there were two bad men. One was a Summoner. His job was to punish people who broke the religious laws. The church was very strong, so he had a lot of power. And he used it to make money from poor people who were afraid of him. This Summoner had a red face with large pimples. [3] He stank [4] of garlic and onions. [5] He looked so terrible that children were afraid when they saw him!

The other man was the Pardoner. He had long yellow hair like rats' tails, with no beard. Ugh! If people gave him money, he forgave them in the name of the Church. That was his job. He always carried bits of wood and cloth and bones which he said came from the Virgin Mary or Jesus or the saints. He was a liar, of course. He earned far more money than the honest Parson. When he sang in church, he had a fine voice. But his heart was black and ugly.

---

1. **wart** : a large growth on the skin.

2. **bagpipes** : a musical instrument.

3. **pimples** : red spots on the face.

4. **stank** (*stink, stank, stunk*): smelled very badly.

5. **garlic and onions** : strong-smelling vegetables.

The Prologue

There were many other pilgrims. But it will be boring if I tell you about them all. It's time to begin telling the stories.

I shall tell you everything about the pilgrimage. But please remember that I am only repeating what the pilgrims said and did. If sometimes the stories which they told are not polite, it's not my fault. [1] I must tell the truth, mustn't I?

So, the pilgrims began their journey from The Tabard Inn on the south bank of the Thames. Before we left, the Host [2] gave us all a great meal. After we had eaten, he spoke to us. He was a large, bright-eyed man, who loved to have fun.

'Welcome, ladies and gentlemen. I have decided to come with you to visit Saint Thomas. I hope we all enjoy our journey to Canterbury. I have an idea which will help us to enjoy the long pilgrimage. Each person must tell a story on the way to Canterbury. And another story on the way back! We'll give a prize to the person who tells the best story. What do you think?'

All the pilgrims agreed with this idea. They ordered more wine and then went to bed. Early next morning, the Host woke everybody up.

'Who will tell the first story?' he asked. 'I choose the Knight.'

'Very well,' said the Knight. 'I will begin the game. Let's start riding towards Canterbury — and listen to my story.'

---

1. **fault** : responsibility.
2. **Host** : the owner of the inn.

The text and **beyond**

1 Spot the difference

Listen to the beginning of The Prologue, which is told this time with ten changes from the correct version in Part One. How many of the changes can you identify from memory, without looking back to pages 15-16?

FCE 2 Characters

For each question below choose from the people (A-K). The people may be chosen more than once. When more than one answer is required, these may be given in any order. There is an example at the beginning (0).

A the Countryman	**E** the Knight	**I** the Friar
B Geoffrey Chaucer	**F** the Prioress	**J** the Squire
C the Monk	**G** the Summoner	**K** the Wife of Bath
D the Pardoner	**H** the Merchant	

Which person:

0 [B] was already staying at the Tabard Inn?

1 ☐ was sincere, polite and modest?

2 ☐ had fought in war for love?

3 ☐ was a true man of the forest?

4 ☐ spoke French?

5 ☐ loved pretty girls and drinking?

6 ☐ loved the world?

7 ☐ had been married five times?

8 ☐ ☐ were bad men?

9 ☐ ☐ ☐ were rich?

3 Discussion

Which of the pilgrims do you think Chaucer most admires? Which does he most dislike? Give your reasons.

'... they go to Canterbury to visit the tomb of Thomas Becket, the martyr, who helped the sick.'

The relative pronouns **who, which, whose** and **where** are used to make non-defining relative clauses, which link sentences. For example:

The Miller bought corn. He turned this corn into flour.

*The Miller bought corn, **which** he turned into flour.*

The Prioress was the head of a Priory. Nuns lived and worked in this kind of place.

*The Prioress was the head of a Priory, **where** nuns lived and worked.*

4 **Non-defining relative clauses**

Match sentences 1-7 with sentences A-G. Then use relative pronouns to combine each pair of sentences into one sentence. Write them down.

1 ☐ The Wife of Bath had been married five times.
2 ☐ Chaucer wrote *The Canterbury Tales*.
3 ☐ Pilgrimages usually began in April.
4 ☐ The Prioress had several little dogs.
5 ☐ The Pardoner and the Summoner were bad men.
6 ☐ Chaucer stayed at the Tabard Inn.
7 ☐ The Knight was a perfect gentleman.

A The pilgrims started their journey at the Tabard Inn.
B She was an expert in love.
C April is the first month of spring.
D They took money from the poor.
E His son was adored by all the girls.
F She loved them.
G He lived in the fourteenth century.

5 Vocabulary – describing people

When Chaucer presents the Prioress to us he describes her clothes (a cloak) and her jewellery (her brooch, bracelet and beads). This could be just to give us a nice visual picture. Or there could be another reason. What do you think? Remember, the Prioress should be a very religious person...

6 Divide these thirty words into five groups of six words each.

attractive   beard   blonde   blouse   bracelet   brooch
cloak   curly   ear-rings   elegant   elbow   finger   graceful
hat   handsome   hips   jacket   knee   moustache   necklace
overcoat   pendant   pretty   ring   straight   skirt   thumb
ugly   wavy   wrist

Jewellery	Hair	Clothes	Appearance adjectives	Parts of the body

7 Add three words to each list. Has the rest of the class thought of the same words as you?

8 Discussion

Chaucer often suggests a pilgrim's character by describing his/her appearance. Do you ever form an idea of someone's character from what they look like and/or what they wear? Should we do this?

T: GRADE 7

9 **Speaking – village and country life**
Look closely at the photograph, taken about a hundred years ago, of middle-class Americans dressed up for a special event in April (a social event in spring, as in *The Canterbury Tales*!). Use a dictionary to look for any words you need to know, and use the structure *used to* to talk about the fashions you can see. For example:

It's April, but the people are wearing quite a lot of clothes, so it seems people used to wear more clothes then. They didn't use to dress informally. Men used to wear hats.

Now continue, trying to talk about as many details as you can.

Fashionable spectators at a horse-riding event on the east coast of the USA, April 1913.

10 Society then and now

A   Chaucer's twenty-nine pilgrims (we have shown you twenty-two, plus Chaucer himself and the host) give us a good picture of fourteenth-century English society. Chaucer chose them from all levels of society (except royalty and the extremely poor) in order to represent society as a whole. Think of the characters in Part One again. How many are connected with organised religion? How many are women? Would these numbers be the same today?

B   Create a group of modern travellers to represent society now. We can imagine a similar setting: Waterloo railway station is south of the River Thames, only a couple of kilometres to the west of where the Tabard Inn was. From here the Eurostar train leaves for Paris, passing through the county of Kent, where Canterbury is. Imagine that the train has been delayed, and twenty-nine people are waiting in the Eurostar lounge at Waterloo.

In small groups think of twenty-nine people with different jobs/positions in society — with a mixture of ages, sexes and ethnic backgrounds — that reflect modern society. Compare your ideas in class.

11 Writing

Choose one or two of your travellers and write a short paragraph to describe them. Chaucer exaggerated his characters, and you can do this too! For example, a businessperson might be described like this:

The Businessman was in his fifties. He had hard eyes, and never smiled. He was wearing a blue suit, and every five minutes or so he made a phone call. He had computer printouts of sales figures in his hand, which he kept looking at anxiously. He told us about his important meetings with top business people that he was going to have in Paris.

If you like, you can use some of the faces below to give you ideas, or just use your own mental ideas of your travellers. Think about:

age   physical appearance   clothes   what they had with them
if they were eating or drinking   what they did
what they said   any other details

Before you read

1 Reading pictures

Look at the picture on page 31. Where are the men? Do you think that they know the woman?

PART TWO

The Knight's Tale

alamon and Arcite were two cousins who lived in the Greek city of Thebes. The King of Thebes, Creon, was an old, wicked [1] man who treated his enemies very badly. Theseus, the Duke of Athens, met a group of women as he was travelling. They were crying.

'Help us, Lord Theseus. We are all widows. [2] Creon has murdered our husbands!'

Theseus decided to attack Thebes. He sent his wife, Hippolyta, and her sister, Emily, to his palace, where they would be safe. Then he marched towards Thebes with his soldiers.

Palamon and Arcite fought bravely to defend their city but, in the end, they fell unconscious [3] to the ground. The victorious soldiers of Athens walked among the dead bodies on the battlefield. [4]

---

1. **wicked** [wɪkɪd] : very bad.
2. **widows** : women whose husbands are dead.
3. **unconscious** : without feeling anything.
4. **battlefield** : the place where a battle takes place.

'Come here!' shouted a soldier. 'These two are still breathing. They're alive!'

It was Palamon and Arcite. Theseus took the two young men prisoner. He took them back to Athens and locked them in a tall dark tower. No gold could buy their freedom. They were prisoners for life!

One morning in May, Emily, the sister of Queen Hippolyta, was walking in the garden near the tower. She was as beautiful as the lilies [1] and roses that grew there. She sang like an angel. Palamon, who was looking sadly out of the window, cried out when he saw her. An arrow had gone through his heart. He had fallen in love.

Arcite heard him shout. He also came to the window and looked out through the thick iron bars. [2] As soon as he saw Emily, he also lost his heart to her. They were both in love with the same woman!

Palamon was angry with Arcite. 'You are my friend and my cousin. When we were children, we promised that we would always help each other. Now you have betrayed [3] me! You are in love with my lady!'

'I love her more than you,' replied Arcite. 'I am right to love her. There is no law in love. But let's stop quarrelling. [4] We are both prisoners. She will never marry either of us.'

1. **lilies** : beautiful white flowers.

2. **the thick iron bars** :

3. **betrayed** : broken your promise.

4. **quarrelling** : fighting with words.

Every day the two cousins, with burning hearts, looked through the bars and watched her walking in the garden.

Shortly after this, a duke from Thebes came to visit Duke Theseus. This visitor was a friend of Arcite and begged [1] Theseus to release him from prison. 'I will pay you money,' he said.

Duke Theseus spoke sternly. [2] 'I agree to let him go. But there is one condition. Arcite must leave Athens immediately. If he ever returns, he will die!'

So Arcite received his freedom but had to return to Thebes while Palamon remained in the tower all alone.

Arcite was very unhappy. 'I am free but I cannot see the lovely Emily. Palamon is far luckier than I am. Every day, he can look out of his window and watch her walking in the garden. He is in Paradise!' [3]

Palamon was equally unhappy. 'Arcite is far luckier than I am. He can collect a great army in Thebes and march against Athens. If he wins the war against Theseus, he can marry Emily. He is in Paradise!'

Arcite, however, had a different plan. He came back secretly to Athens. He looked pale and sick because he had been suffering [4] for so long from a broken heart. Nobody recognised him. He took off his lord's clothes and put on the clothes of a poor man. Then he went to the house of Lady Emily.

'My name is Philostrate,' he told the servants. 'I am looking for a job.'

---

1. **begged** : asked very much.
2. **sternly** : seriously.
3 **Paradise** : some people think it a wonderful place you go to after you die; (here) a beautiful place.
4. **suffering** : having a very bad time.

He was a strong, hard-working young man, so he was given a job. Arcite became the personal servant of Lady Emily! But if anyone recognised him, he would die.

Palamon was in the tower for seven years. One day, however, a friend helped him to escape. He gave the guard a glass of wine with drugs in it that made him sleep. Then Palamon ran away. He crept [1] through Athens in the middle of the night and reached the countryside, where he hid in a grove. [2] Both lovers were now free.

It was May. All the fields were green, the flowers were brightly coloured and the birds were singing. Thinking about his love for Emily, Arcite rode into the countryside.

'I am in a terrible situation,' he said aloud, thinking that no one was listening. 'I cannot use my real name. I am only a servant to the lady that I want to make my wife.'

Palamon was hiding nearby in the forest. When he heard Arcite, he was very angry and rushed towards him.

'Emily is mine!' he shouted. 'You must not love her.'

'You are a lunatic [3] for love,' said Arcite.

The two cousins began fighting, like a lion and a tiger in the forest, until they were standing in a river of blood.

On the same day, Theseus woke up early in his palace in the city. 'It is a clear, bright day. We'll go hunting,' he decided. He rode out into the countryside with Hippolyta, his lovely queen, and her sister, Emily. Suddenly, he saw two men fighting like animals in the middle of the forest.

'Stop!' he shouted. 'Who are you?'

1. **crept** : (*creep/crept/crept*) moved quietly and secretly.
2. **grove** : a small group of trees.
3. **lunatic** : mad person.

'I am Palamon,' replied one. 'I deserve to die. I have escaped from your prison. But this is Arcite. He also deserves to die. He has returned to Athens from Thebes under the name of Philostrate. We are fighting because we both love the lady Emily. Kill us both at the same time!'

'Yes, you deserve to die,' said Theseus. 'You are the enemies of Athens.'

But Emily and her ladies begged Theseus not to kill them. 'They are young, handsome men from good families. Forgive them.'

Theseus thought carefully. 'A good king must not be angry. He must be calm and wise. The God of Love is very powerful. Instead of escaping to Thebes, Palamon and Arcite stayed here because they loved you, Emily, even though you didn't know anything about their love! I was a lover when I was young. I have also done stupid things for love. I will let them live.'

He turned to Palamon and Arcite. 'Only one of you can marry my sister-in-law. Go away and collect a hundred knights each. In a year's time, return to Athens. Your two armies will fight and the winner will be the husband of Emily.'

The two cousins were very happy. They knelt in front of Theseus and thanked him. Then they returned as quickly as possible to Thebes. A year later, they came back to Athens. Each rode at the head of a hundred knights. [1] The people of Athens came out into the streets to watch.

Arcite prayed to Mars, the god of war, and Palamon prayed for the help of Venus, the goddess of love. Arcite's men carried the red flag of Mars and Palamon's men carried the white flag of Venus.

The fighting lasted from morning until night but finally Arcite

---

1 . **rode … knights** : had a hundred knights on horse following him.

and his hundred knights gained the victory. Mars had won! 'Arcite will marry Emily,' announced Theseus.

In Heaven, among the gods and goddesses, Venus was very angry. 'I am the Queen of Love but I have lost.'

She looked down on the world and saw Arcite riding on his horse towards Emily to take her as his wife. They looked softly at each other. Women usually love the winner. But then Venus acted. Suddenly, there was an earth tremor. [1] The ground shook [2] under Arcite's horse. The horse was frightened and threw Arcite to the ground. He fell from his saddle and was badly injured.

They carried Arcite to his bed and sent for doctors. 'Emily! Emily!' he called. The doctors tried to save him but he knew that he would die. Palamon and Emily came to his bedside.

'Oh Lady Emily, I love you greatly. You are my heart's queen. Take me in your arms and listen to me carefully. I am sorry now that I quarrelled with Palamon, who loves you too. After I die, if you wish to marry, think of him.'

He looked into Emily's eyes. Then he died.

There was a great funeral. Arcite's body was placed in a great fire just as, in his life, he had burnt in the fire of love.

Emily and Palamon were both very sad. They had lost a husband, a cousin and a friend.

'Out of two sorrows, make one perfect joy,' said Theseus. 'Marry each other, as Arcite wished.'

So Emily and Palamon got married and lived all the rest of their lives in great happiness.

'And that is the end of my tale,' said the Knight.

---

1. **earth tremor** : a shaking of the land, a small earthquake.
2. **shook** : (*shake, shook, shaken*) moved quickly.

The text and **beyond**

1 Comprehension check

Answer the following questions. Try to answer from memory; look back at the text only if you really need to.

1 Why did Theseus attack Thebes?

2 Where did Theseus put Palamon and Arcite?

3 Why did Palamon and Arcite quarrel?

4 Why did Arcite return to Athens?

5 How did Palamon become free?

6 What did the cousins do in the forest?

7 Why didn't Theseus kill Palamon and Arcite?

8 How many knights came to the battle?

9 Who won the battle?

10 Who married Emily?

FCE **2 Summary**

Read the summary below and think of the word which best fits each space. Use only one word in each space. There is an example at the beginning (**0**).

Palamon and Arcite were two cousins (**0**) ..who............ lived in the Greek city of Thebes. When Theseus, (**1**) .... Duke of Athens, attacked their city, Palamon and Arcite fought bravely but in the (**2**) .... they were taken prisoner, taken back to Athens and locked in a tower.

One day Emily, the sister of Hippolyta, Theseus's wife, (**3**) .... walking in the garden near the tower. She was very beautiful and when Palamon and Arcite saw her they (**4**) .... fell in love with her and began arguing (**5**) .... who should marry her.

Soon after, Arcite was freed (**6**) .... condition that he left Athens. However, he came (**7**) .... secretly to Athens and found a job in Emily's house. After seven years Palamon escaped (**8**) .... the tower and arrived in the countryside. There he met Arcite, who was out riding. The two cousins began fighting for Emily until Theseus arrived (9) .... Hippolyta and Emily.

(10) .... first Theseus was very angry but then he told Palamon and Arcite to go away and collect 100 knights (11) .... and then return to Athens to fight. The winner would then marry Emily. Arcite won the (12) .... but, as he approached Emily, he was thrown from (13) .... horse. As he lay dying he told Palamon and Emily to (14) .... married. They (15) .... very sad, but after the funeral they got married and lived happily together for the rest of their lives.

Do you think there are any important elements of the story that are missing from this summary?

3 Discussion

A   Who do you think acted more nobly, Palamon or Arcite?

B   What do you think of Theseus's way of deciding which of the cousins can marry Emily? Why does he say a hundred knights instead of fifty or ten? Or why doesn't he suggest another way? In small groups, think of some other ways in which Theseus might have decided who should marry Emily. Compare your ideas in class.

C   Look at these three comments on love:

  • 'There is no law in love' (Arcite, at the bottom of page 29).

  • 'You are a lunatic for love' (Arcite, on page 32).

  • 'Amor vincit omnia' — 'Love conquers all' (on the Prioress's brooch, page 18).

  Which of these comments do you think applies best to the story? Can you think of another comment on love which applies to the story?

D   The story puts love and friendship in competition. Can you think of an alternative ending which very clearly shows that either love or friendship is stronger?

4 Vocabulary – fighting words

Here is an English proverb, a traditional saying. Each number represents a letter of the alphabet.

1.2.'3.	4.5.2.2.5.6.	2.7.	8.9.10.5.	11.7.10.5.12.
9.13.12.	11.7.3.2.	2.8.9.13.	13.5.10.5.6.	2.7.
8.9.10.5.	11.7.10.5.12.	9.2.	9.11.11.	

If you can find the words below, you will be able to find the proverb. All the words are connected with fighting. Use a dictionary if necessary.

A	A sport which needs big gloves.	4. 7. **X** 1. 13. **G**
B	Another sport where you fight.	W 6. 5. 3. 2. 11. 1. 13. **G**
C	The winner.	C. 8. 9. **M P** 1. 7. 13.
D	The winning side can celebrate this.	10. 1. **C** 2. 7. 6. **Y**
E	The opposite of this is...	12. 5. **F** 5. 9. 2.
F	Guns, knives, swords are all...	W 5. 9. **P** 7. 13. 3.
G	Waterloo was a very important...	4. 9. 2. 2. 11. 5.
H	An agreement to end a war.	2. 6. 5. 9. 2. **Y**
I	These people fight on the land.	2. 8. 5. 9. 6. **M Y**
J	These people fight on the sea.	2. 8. 5. 13. 9. 10. **Y**
K	These people fight in the sky.	2. 8. 5. 9. 1. 6. **F** 7. 6. **C** 5.
L	In a war, the opposite side is the...	5. 13. 5. **M Y**
M	A football team must have a good...	9. 2. 2. 9. **C K**
N	It also needs a good...	12. 5. **F** 5. 13. **C** 5.
O	The opposite of 'war'.	P 5. 9. **C** 5.
P	The Knight is a...	3. 7. 11. 12. 1. 5. 6.

Write the proverb here:

__ ' _ _____ __ ____ _____ ___   ____ ____

_____ __ ____ _____ __ ___.

Do you agree with this proverb? Do you have a similar proverb in your language?

5 **Proverbs**

Here are some more common English proverbs. What values do they teach? Are there similar proverbs in your language?

1   Too many cooks spoil the broth ('broth' = soup).

2   An apple a day keeps the doctor away.

3   Many hands make light work.

4   It's no use crying over spilt milk.

5   People who live in glass houses shouldn't throw stones.

6   Rome wasn't built in a day.

6 *The Miller's Tale*

FCE

You will hear part of *The Miller's Tale*. For questions 1-10, tick (✓) the correct box, true (T) or false (F).

		T	F
1	The carpenter[1] was a clever man.	☐	☐
2	Nicholas was a lodger[2] in the house.	☐	☐
3	Nicholas had a dream about a flood.[3]	☐	☐
4	He told the carpenter about his 'dream'.	☐	☐
5	Alison drowned[4] in the flood.	☐	☐
6	The carpenter made three large boats.	☐	☐
7	He put the boats in the roof.	☐	☐
8	They all slept inside the boats.	☐	☐
9	It rained for several weeks.	☐	☐
10	Nicholas's trick was successful.	☐	☐

1.   **carpenter** : man who works with wood.
2.   **lodger** : someone who pays to stay in another person's home.
3.   **flood** [flʌd] : a natural disaster when the water covers the land.
4.   **drowned** : died in the water.

7 Fill in the gaps

Read the passage below and fill in the gaps with a suitable preposition. Choose from these prepositions, which you can use more than once:

at	by	in	for	from	of	through	to	with

Chaucer gives each (**1**) .... his pilgrims a story which is suitable (**2**) .... their character. (**3**) .... example, the noble Knight tells a story that comes (**4**) .... the 'courtly love' tradition, which was started (**5**) .... poets in the south of France (**6**) .... the 1100s and spread (**7**) .... Europe. (**8**) .... the 'courtly love' tradition, a noble man falls (**9**) .... love (**10**) .... a woman who he cannot have, either because she is a long way away or married (**11**) .... another man. The lover suffers and prays a lot (**12**) .... the god of love, but he stays faithful (**13**) .... his love, and always tries to act (**14**) .... a noble way. The miller, who is drunk (**15**) .... the time he tells his story, has a story which (**16**) .... a way makes fun (**17**) .... the 'courtly love' tradition. His story is also intended to make fun (**18**) .... the carpenter, one (**19**) .... the pilgrims who the miller doesn't like (**20**) .... all.

8 Speaking

What similarities and differences can you see between *The Knight's Tale* and *The Miller's Tale*?

FCE 9 Writing

Imagine that you are Palamon, locked in the tower, and that you have managed to secretly send out a letter to a friend. Write your letter in 120-180 words in an appropriate style. Include the following:

- seeing Emily
- the quarrel with Arcite
- Arcite's release

- the lonely time in prison
- the plan to escape
- hopes for the future

Thomas Becket

Thomas Becket (sometimes called Thomas à Becket) was murdered on 29 December 1170, in Canterbury Cathedral. This was the end of Becket's life but the beginning of the great tradition of pilgrimage to

Canterbury, which Chaucer writes about in *The Canterbury Tales*. There are many other pieces of literature connected with Becket, including the play *Murder in the Cathedral* by T. S. Eliot (1888-1965).

Becket was born in 1118 in London. As a child, he showed 'quick understanding' and received a good education. He began a career in the Church as an administrator but, in 1154, he became Chancellor [1] to King Henry II. This was one of the most powerful and important jobs in the kingdom. King Henry was twenty-one years old and became great friends

Henry II (1133-1189) from Matthew Paris's *Chronicles*.

---

1. **Chancellor** : the person responsible for money, taxes etc. in the whole country.

with Thomas. For that reason, he appointed him as Archbishop [1] of Canterbury, the head of the Church in all England, in 1162.

But Becket changed. Instead of supporting the King, he defended the power of the Church. There was a long period of disagreement between Henry and Thomas. Finally, Henry became so angry that Becket escaped to France, where he stayed for six years. In 1170, he returned to England. The people of Canterbury welcomed him back to the city and he became a popular hero. He continued to attack the power of the King.

When Henry, who was in France, heard of Thomas's activities, he said angrily: 'Who will rid me of this turbulent priest?' [2] Four knights immediately set off for England. They arrived in Canterbury and looked for Thomas. His monks begged him to lock himself in the cathedral but Becket said that the house of God must remain open. The knights entered the cathedral and killed the Archbishop with axes [3] and swords.

After the murder, King Henry showed his sorrow by coming to Canterbury. He walked barefoot through the city and was whipped [4] by the monks. He was the first pilgrim to Canterbury. After this, pilgrims came from all over England and from other parts of Europe to visit the tomb of Becket. The Pope made him a saint and his tomb was placed at the east end of the cathedral, decorated with jewels. There were many stories of miracles, of sick people who were made well and even of dead people who came alive again because of the power of Saint Thomas.

---

1. **Archbishop** : the top person in the Church of the whole country.
2. **Who will ... turbulent priest?** : Will someone please take this trouble-making priest away from me?
3. **axe** : a sharp instrument or weapon.
4. **whipped** : beaten with whips.

Soon after Henry VIII created the Church of England and broke away from the Catholic Church of Rome, Becket's shrine [1] was destroyed in 1538, and Henry took all the wealth of the monks of Canterbury for the state; it was so much it had to be taken away in twenty-six wagons. Becket's bones, which were buried in the eastern part of the cathedral, were lost after 1538. Today, however, you can still see the place where Becket was murdered. The stories of his miracles are shown in the ancient stained glass windows [2] and there is a famous window which shows a portrait of Becket himself.

Saint **Thomas Becket** in a stained glass window in Canterbury cathedral.

1. **shrine** : a special place where people come to show respect.
2. **stained glass windows** : windows with pictures made of coloured glass (the illustration on this page is an example).

1 Comprehension check

Answer the following questions.

1 At what age did Becket become Archbishop of Canterbury?
2 How did he behave when he got this job? And how did the king and the people react to this behaviour?
3 Why didn't Becket hide when the king's knights were arriving?
4 Who was the first pilgrim at Becket's shrine, and how did he behave when he arrived?
5 The shrine became rich, but what happened to its wealth?

 INTERNET PROJECT

Connect to the Internet and go to www.blackcat-cideb.com or www.cideb.it. Insert the title or part of the title of the book into our search engine. Open the page for *The Canterbury Tales*. Click on the Internet project link. Go down the page until you find the title of this book and click on the relevant link for this project.

▶ Find out some more facts about the Bell Barry Tower.
▶ Choose one or two photographs that interest you, and say why.
▶ Follow the links to other abbeys and cathedrals. Find one that interests you, and say why.

Before you read

1 Vocabulary

Look at the picture on page 47. Can you see these parts of the birds?

- comb : this is on the head of the chicken. It is coloured red.
- beak : chickens, and all birds, bite with this.
- feathers : these cover the bodies of chickens and all birds.
- A male chicken (a cock) makes the noise 'Cock-a-doodle-doo!' in English. What does it make in your language?

PART THREE

The Nun's Priest's Tale

e need a happy tale,' said the Host, 'something to make us laugh.' He saw the Nun's Priest hiding in the background. [1] 'Come, sir, tell us a tale. Your horse is thin and sick but I'm sure that you can tell a good story.'

'I will try to please you,' said the Priest. 'Now listen to my tale...'

Many years ago, in the magic time when all the birds and animals could speak and sing — or so I've heard — there was a poor widow [2] who lived with her two daughters. She had three pigs, three cows and a sheep. She was a simple, patient woman who worked hard and thanked God each day.

In her farmyard, she kept a cock called Chanticleer. He was well-known in the neighbourhood. His crowing [3] was more regular than a clock or a church bell. He was a very handsome

---

1. **in the background** : behind the other pilgrims.
2. **widow** : a woman whose husband has died.
3. **crowing** : making the sound of a cockerel, 'Cock-a-doodle-doo!'

bird. He had a red comb on his head, a shining black beak, blue legs and golden feathers which shone [1] like fire. He was the best and proudest cockerel that has ever lived.

There were seven hens [2] in the yard with Chanticleer. The prettiest was called Lady Pertelote. She was polite, friendly and wise. She had loved Chanticleer since she was a seven-day-old chick and she was his favourite wife. When the sun rose in the morning, the two birds sang a love song together. It was a golden time!

But one day, while he was sleeping in the middle of his seven wives, just before the sun rose, Chanticleer began to scream.

'Darling husband,' Pertelote said, 'what's the matter?'

'Madam,' he replied, 'I have had a terrible dream. I dreamt that a horrible monster wanted to catch me and eat me. He was between yellow and red in colour. There were black tips [3] on his ears and tail. His bright eyes were fixed on me. His rows of teeth were sharp and white.'

'Don't be so afraid,' said Pertelote. 'You have lost my love! I cannot love a coward. [4] All women want strong, independent husbands, not cowards who are afraid of dreams.'

'But the dream is from God,' said Chanticleer.

'Nonsense! Dreams are nothing. All the best writers from the old times agree with me,' said the hen. 'Dreams are the result of eating too much late at night. That is all. Go to the chemist and get

---

1. **shone** : (*shine/shone/shone*) gave bright light.
2. **hens** : female chickens.
3. **tips** : the ends, e.g. fingertips.
4. **coward** : somebody who is always afraid, not brave.

some medicine for your stomach. I'll find you some delicious, fresh worms [1] to eat. Swallow [2] them alive! After a day or two, you will have no more bad dreams. Trust your wife, dear Chanticleer.'

'Thank you, Madam,' said the cock, 'for your advice. But you are wrong. Listen to this story.'

Then Chanticleer told a story to prove that dreams come true.

'Once,' he began, 'there were two men who visited another town on a pilgrimage. There was a great crowd of pilgrims and it was difficult to find a place to stay in the town. So they decided to sleep in separate inns. During the night, one of the men had a dream. His friend was calling out to him. "Please help me! Thieves have murdered me. Look at the blood on my clothes and face. They've stolen my money and hidden my body in a dung cart. [3] Tomorrow morning, come to the west gate of the city. You'll find me there."'

Chanticleer paused. 'It was a horrible dream, full of blood and terror, but the man went back to sleep until the morning. When he woke up, he went to meet his friend at the other inn. But the innkeeper told him that his friend had gone. Quickly, he ran to the west gate of the city. He saw a dung cart leaving the town. So he called the sheriff [4] and asked him to search the cart.

'Is it necessary to tell you the end of the story, dear Pertelote? They found the murdered man in the cart. Murder will always come into the open.

'There are many other stories about dreams, my dear wife.

---

1. **worms** : small creatures that live in the earth.
2. **Swallow** : eat quickly without biting, e.g. swallow medicine.
3. **dung cart** : a wagon for taking away dirt.
4. **sheriff** : the person responsible for the law in the town.

They must be true. You can read them in the best books, even the Bible! So don't call me a coward.

'And now, Madam, the sun is rising. Come to me and let us enjoy ourselves together. It is time for love.'

With these words, Chanticleer forgot the dream and flew down into the yard and all his hens flew after him.

'Look at the great sun in the sky!' Chanticleer crowed. 'Cock-a-doodle-doo! It's the beginning of spring, my seven wives. Oh Madam Pertelote, your beauty fills my heart. When I see how beautiful you are, I'm not afraid. Cock-a-doodle-doo!'

But happiness always ends in sadness. There was a sly [1] fox with black tips on his ears and tail in the yard, under the vegetables, hiding like a murderer. He lay there until the middle of the day, waiting for the right time to run out and catch Chanticleer, the fat cock. He fixed his bright eyes on the delicious-looking bird.

The cock followed his wife's advice. He ate some worms and walked proudly about the yard. Women are the reason for all the bad luck in the world. At least, that's what certain writers say. Not me. I don't believe it myself. Do you?

Pertelote and her sisters were lying in the warm sunlight. They washed their feathers and talked softly about love and food. Chanticleer walked freely and happily in the widow's farmyard, picking up worms and pieces of corn. Then suddenly, he saw the fox. It was the first time he had ever seen a fox but he was immediately afraid.

'Sir,' said the fox, 'why are you running away? I am your great friend and admirer. I came here especially to hear you sing. I knew

---

1. **sly** : clever, in a secret way.

your father and mother. They also had wonderful voices. They gave me great pleasure, especially when they came to my home.'

Chanticleer was very happy and proud. The stranger liked his singing!

The stupid bird stood on his toes. He pushed up his neck towards the sky, puffed up [1] his chest, closed his eyes and opened his black, shining beak. He began to sing. But not for long!

It was all over [2] in a second!

The fox jumped. He caught Chanticleer by the neck, threw him over his back, and ran off towards the forest.

It was a terrible thing! Why had Chanticleer flown down into the yard? Why hadn't he stayed on the roof where he was safe? Why had his wife not believed in dreams? This great bird, the husband of seven wives, the handsomest creature in the world, the beautiful singer of morning love songs, was going to die! Greece lost its power. Rome burned. And Chanticleer, the cockerel, was stolen by a fox!

Pertelote and the hens screamed loudly. The widow ran out of her house and saw the fox. He was running towards the trees with Chanticleer over his shoulder. It was too late to stop him.

The widow, her two daughters, her servants with sticks, four dogs, the cook, the maid, even the cows, the sheep and the pigs, all ran after the fox and Chanticleer the cockerel. Ducks flew up out of the pond, quacking. Bees buzzed in the air in a great swarm. [3] The men blew trumpets and shouted like a great army. The earth shook and the sky seemed to fall.

---

1. **puffed up** : filled with air, made larger.
2. **it was all over** : it was finished.
3. **swarm** : a group of bees.

Now, Chanticleer's luck changed.

Chanticleer spoke to the fox as they arrived in the forest. The fox's teeth were sharply round his neck but he could just talk. 'You are safe now, sir. These stupid people who are running after us will never catch you. Turn round and shout at them. "You idiots, I'm cleverer than all of you! Did you think you could catch Reynard the fox? You can't stop me now. I'll eat this cock for my supper." Then they will respect you, sir.'

The fox answered. 'Yes, you're right.' He opened his mouth and spoke. 'Idiots! I'm cleverer than all of you. I'll eat this... .'

But as soon as Reynard opened his mouth, Chanticleer got free. He flew high into the trees and sat on a branch looking down at the fox.

'Oh, Chanticleer,' called the fox, 'why have you flown away? Did I frighten you? I'm sorry, sir. Come down and I'll explain. I wasn't going to eat you — I simply wanted to bring you to my home so that you could sing for me and my children.'

'No,' said the cock, 'I won't be a fool twice. I'll never close my eyes and sing again when there's a fox in the yard!'

'And I'll never open my mouth to speak empty words,' said the fox.

'And that is the end of my tale,' said the Nun's Priest. 'It's only a story of a fox, a cock and a hen but we can all learn a lesson from it.'

'It was a good story,' agreed the Host. 'Don't you wish you had seven wives, like the cock? But you're a priest and can have none.'

The text and **beyond**

1 Comprehension check

Answer the following questions. Try to answer from memory; look back at the text only if you really need to.

1 Where did Chanticleer live?
2 How many 'wives' did Chanticleer have, and who was his favourite?
3 What did Chanticleer dream about?
4 Chanticleer and his favourite wife disagreed about dreams: how?
5 How did the fox catch Chanticleer?
6 What did the fox do when he had got Chanticleer, and what did everyone else do?
7 How did Chanticleer escape?
8 The fox tried to get Chanticleer again after he had escaped: how? Did he succeed?

2 The moral

The 'moral' of a story is what we learn from it about how we should or should not behave. The narrator of this story, the Nun's Priest (a member of the Prioress's group), says at the end of his story: 'It's only a story of a fox, a cock and a hen but we can all learn a lesson from it.' In pairs or small groups write a moral to this story in no more than 12 words. Use a dictionary if necessary. Compare your ideas in class and try to agree.

3 Characters

Chanticleer, Pertelote, Reynard the fox: who did you like most? Why?

4 Discussion

A Look again at the description of the fox stealing Chanticleer in the middle of page 50. Do you think this is funny or not? (You will find some information about this kind of description in exercise 9, but don't look yet).

B Do you think this story is against women, in favour of women, or neither?

5 Past Simple and Past Perfect Simple

Complete the following sentences. In each of the gaps use one verb
from the box in the Past Simple and one verb in the Past Perfect
Simple.

> be   come   fly   have   love   open   finish   reach
>
> recover   steal   stop   try   tell (x2)   thank   walk

A After he .... from the shock of the dream, he ....
around the farmyard.

B The fox .... running when he .... the forest.

C Pertelote .... Chanticleer since she .... a young
chick.

D One morning, Chanticleer .... his wife that he ....
a terrible dream.

E Chanticleer .... up into the trees after the fox ....
his mouth.

F The fox .... Chanticleer that he .... to the
farmyard to hear him sing.

G After the priest .... his tale, the Host .... him.

H Everyone .... to catch the fox who ....
Chanticleer.

6 Summary

Put the sentences in exercise 5 in the order they happen in the story.
Write the numbers 1-8 in the boxes:

A ☐   B ☐   C ☐   D ☐   E ☐   F ☐   G ☐   H ☐

Is there anything important missing from this summary? Write 2 or 3
sentences which describe events that you think are important, and
put them in the right place among the boxes above.

7 **The dream of drowning**

FCE

You will hear Chanticleer telling another story about a dream. For questions 1-10 complete the sentences.

1 Chanticleer told Pertelote some more ....

2 Two merchants wanted to cross ....

3 They waited in the port until the ....

4 One of the travellers was worried because he had ....

5 He wanted to ....

6 His friend said that he wasn't afraid ....

7 The friend decided to go to France and ....

8 But during the journey there was ....

9 The ship sank and every ....

10 If Pertelote knew more history she wouldn't ....

8 **Dreams**

A Like Chanticleer, people used to think that dreams told us what would happen in the future. Nowadays, what do people think that dreams are? If necessary, use encyclopedias or the Internet.

B What do you think the word 'dream' means in the following contexts? If necessary, use a dictionary.

- *I have a dream*: repeated many times in a famous speech by the black American human rights activist Martin Luther King (1929-68).

- *I'm dreaming of a white Christmas*: a line from a very famous popular song (*White Christmas*, 1942).

- *the dream team*: the name given to the USA basketball team of 1992.

C Find some other quotations with the word 'dream' in them and share them with the class.

D Write three sentences about yourself using the word 'dream'.

9 **Fables with animals**

A fable is a short story, sometimes in poetry, which has a moral at the end of it. The characters are usually animals who talk and behave like humans. According to tradition, the first fables we have were written by a Greek slave called Aesop in the sixth century BC, although these fables probably came from different places.

Fables were popular in the Middle Ages, and there was also a development of the fable called the 'beast epic', where the style of writing is similar to the serious style of epic poetry, often to make the story funny. A series of stories like this, found in several European languages, was about Reynard the Fox, who plays tricks on other characters. Chaucer based *The Nun's Priest's Tale* on one of these stories. Perhaps Walt Disney's cartoon film *Robin Hood* (1973), with a fox as Robin Hood, is in the tradition of the Reynard the Fox stories.

The Frenchman Jean de La Fontaine's Fables (1668 -1694) are generally considered classics, and while Rudyard Kipling's *Just So Stories* (1902) are very amusing, George Orwell's *Animal Farm* (1945) is a serious satire on Communism as it developed in Russia under Stalin.

Films with talking animals have been popular ever since the first Mickey Mouse cartoon, *Steamboat Willie* (1928). Although cartoons with animals are often comic, some can be quite serious too, such as *The Lion King* (1994). There have also been animal films that are not cartoons, such as *Babe* (1995) and its sequel *Babe – Pig in the City* (1998).

1   Are there fables with animals in your culture? Do they have morals?

2   Make a list in class of cartoons with animals that you have seen. Which one(s) does the class prefer? Why?

FCE **10** **A Nigerian fable**

This fable originates from the Igbo language of south-eastern Nigeria; about 18 million people speak this language. Read the fable and think of the word which best fits each space. Use only one word in each space. There is an example at the beginning (0).

Once upon a time, all the animals were (**0**) .....invited.......... to an important meeting. As they arrived (**1**) .... the square early in the morning, one of (**2**) ...., the cock was seen by his neighbours going (**3**) .... the opposite direction. 'Why are you going (**4**) .... from the square? Didn't you get the invitation?' they said.

'Yes, I (**5**) ....,' said the cock, 'and I certainly (**6**) .... come to the meeting if I didn't have (**7**) .... important to do at home. Please (**8**) .... my apologies to everyone at the meeting, and say that even (**9**) .... I won't be there in body, I'll be there (**10**) .... spirit! Whatever you decide, you can count (**11**) .... my complete support.'

The reason why the animals (**12**) .... been invited to the meeting was to discuss the problem of man's frequent sacrifice of animals to his gods. In the noisy but short meeting (**13**) .... was decided that they would offer man just one sacrificial animal if he (**14**) .... leave all the others in peace. It was decided (**15**) .... everyone that the cock should be the animal permanently offered to man.

11 In pairs or small groups write a moral to the Igbo fable in exercise 10 in no more than 12 words. Use a dictionary if necessary. Compare your ideas in class and try to agree.

FCE **12** **Writing**
In small groups, think of the names of farm animals. Which group can think of the most names in two minutes? Then choose one or some of the animals and write a short story (120-180 words) in the form of a fable. Give your fable a title. Do not write the moral at the end: ask other groups to guess the moral you thought of.

Before you read

1 **Reading pictures**
Look carefully at the picture on page 65. Do not look at any of the text! Make up a mini-story (just one sentence!) to explain what has happened to lead up to the scene in the picture. Compare your mini-stories in class.

PART FOUR

The Pardoner's Tale

ne day, the Pardoner got drunk and told us all his secrets.

'I go into the churches and speak to the people.

"You are all good people. But if anyone has stolen money from his neighbour or cheated [1] her husband with another man, they will go to Hell. But if you give me money,
I will forgive you in the name of God."

'Then they all hurry to give me gold. Who knows what happens after they die? — I don't care if they go to Heaven or Hell. I just want their money. Even the poor widow has something to give me. I have enough gold to buy a drink of wine and a girl in every town.

'But even a bad man like me can tell a good story. Listen to my tale.'

Some years ago, there was a group of young men who lived very badly. They danced and played music all day long. They

---

1. **cheated** : betrayed, been unfaithful to.

loved eating and drinking, and afterwards they ran after the women of the town. Above all, they loved gambling. [1] They lived in a time of broken promises and lies and swearing. [2]

I am going to tell you about three of these bad young men. One Sunday they were sitting in a tavern, drinking heavily instead of going to church. They heard a bell ringing. In the street, the people were taking a dead man to the churchyard. One of the men called the servant boy. 'Go and find out who has died. Make sure you get his name correctly.'

'I can tell you his name,' said the boy. 'He was one of your friends. But suddenly last night, he was killed. He was sitting at the table, completely drunk, when a silent thief named Death came and stabbed [3] him in the heart. Then the killer went away without a word. Death kills all of us round here. He has killed a thousand during the Plague. Be careful if you meet him, sirs. You see him everywhere you go. That's what my mother told me. It's all I know.'

The host of the tavern agreed. 'The boy's right. This year, Death killed everyone in a large village near here. Every man, woman and child was killed, the lords and the poor men. Death lives not far away. He's always appearing among us.'

'Great God, I'm not afraid!' said one of the young men. 'I'll look for this murderer, Death, in every street. I'll make a promise now. My brothers, let's drink together. We three are one! Death has killed our friends. Now, we will kill him before the day is finished!'

---

1. **gambling** : playing cards etc. for money.
2. **swearing** : (*swear/swore/sworn*) using bad language.
3. **stabbed** : killed with a knife.

The three men stood up and drank. 'We will live and die for one another,' they promised. 'We are all brothers!' They went out of the tavern, completely drunk, and went towards the village where everyone had been killed. 'If we catch him, then Death is dead!'

On the way, they met a very old, very poor man. He was wrapped [1] in old clothes so that they could hardly [2] see his face. He greeted [3] them politely. 'God be with you, my lords.'

'Get out of our way, you old fool,' said the leader of the men. 'Why do you live such a long time? It's time for an old man like you to die!'

'I have been all over the world, as far as India,' said the old man, 'but I cannot find a young man who will change his life for mine. So I live as an old man until God decides that I should die.

'Not even Death will take my life. So, like a prisoner in this world, I wait for my freedom. The earth is my mother. I knock on her gate with my stick and cry "Dear Mother! Let me in! Look at me! I am growing thinner every day. Wrap me in a sheet and take me into my grave!" But she refuses to help me. So my face is white and my bones ache.'

The old man looked at the leader. 'You spoke very rudely to me just now. That is wrong. It says in the Bible that you should respect an old man with white hair. Don't hurt me, but treat me kindly so that, when you are old yourself, people will respect you. Now let me pass. I must go where I must go.'

'No, old fool, you cannot escape from us so easily,' said the leader. 'You spoke about Death a few moments ago. Death has

---

1. **wrapped** : covered.   2. **hardly** : almost not.   3. **greeted** : said 'hello'.

killed all our friends in this place. You are one of his spies! Tell us where he is or you'll pay for it. You are certainly one of Death's gang who plan to kill all the young people. You wicked thief!'

'Well, sirs, if you really want to find Death, follow this crooked[1] path towards that forest. I left him there, under a tree. Can you see the oak?[2] He's waiting for you there, I'm sure. He's not afraid of rude young men like you. Now God be with you and help you to become good.'

The three men ran down the crooked path towards the tree while the old man stood and watched. Then he continued on his journey.

What did they find under the tree? A huge pile of new gold coins![3]

They had never seen so much gold. They immediately forgot all about Death when they saw the shining money. It made them very happy.

The leader spoke first. 'Brothers, listen to me carefully. I have a plan. Luck has given us this treasure so that we can live happily and luxuriously[4] for the rest of our lives. We'll spend it all on pleasure. We didn't expect this to be our lucky day.

'We must take the gold away to my house as soon as possible. Or one of your houses. Brothers, we know that it is our gold. God has given it to us to make us happy. But we mustn't take it by day. People will think we are thieves. They will hang us because of our treasure. We must take it away secretly at night.

---

1. **crooked** [krʊkɪd] : not straight.
2. **oak** : a kind of tree.
3. **coins** : round metal pieces of money.
4. **luxuriously** : in a very comfortable and expensive way.

Therefore, one of us must go to the town to get bread and wine for us all while the others stay and look after the treasure. He must go quickly and secretly. Then, when it is dark, we'll carry the gold to one of our houses. What do you think?'

They all agreed. They drew lots [1] and the youngest ran off to the town to get bread and wine. The other two stayed under the tree with the gold.

As soon as the youngest one had gone, the leader talked to the other. 'You are my true brother. We can help each other. You know that our companion has gone to the town. And here's a huge pile of gold which we will divide among the three of us. But if we divided it between two, that would be better for both of us. Do you agree, friend?'

'That's impossible,' said the other. 'He knows that we have the gold. If we take it all, how can we explain it to him?'

'Do you agree or not?' asked the first one. 'I can tell you my plan in a few words if you're interested.'

'Tell me. I will support you.'

'Well, we are two and he is only one. We are stronger than him. When he comes back, begin to wrestle [2] with him — he'll think it is a game. Then I will come up secretly behind him and stab him in the back while you are fighting. Do the same. Stick your knife in his chest. Then, my dear friend, we will divide all this gold between the two of us, like brothers.'

So these two criminals decided to kill the third one as soon as he returned.

---

1. **drew lots** : (draw/drew/drawn) decided by taking a piece of straw each.
2. **wrestle** : fight as a sport or a game.

But the youngest was also thinking about the gold as he ran to town. The shining coins were beautiful and bright. 'Oh God,' he thought, 'I would like all this gold for myself. No one would be as happy as I would be then.'

The Devil [1] put an idea in his head. 'I'll poison [2] my two companions,' he thought. He did not feel sorry for his friends. He only thought about the gold.

Immediately, he went to a chemist in the town. 'I need some poison to kill rats,' he said. 'Also, there's an animal which is killing my chickens at home. I must poison it.'

The chemist replied, 'I'll give you the strongest poison that I have. There is nobody, man or animal, that can take this poison and live. The smallest bit is enough to kill a man in a few minutes.'

The young man took the box of poison and left. He went to a shop in the next street and bought three bottles. He put the poison in two of the bottles but not in the third. He would drink from that bottle and enjoy the gold after his companions were dead. Then he filled the bottles with wine and went back to the tree.

I am near the end of my story. As they had agreed, the two other men killed the youngest one as soon as he returned with the wine. Then they sat down. 'Now let's sit and drink before we bury his body.'

The leader took one of the bottles, drank, and passed it to his friend who also drank. It was the poisoned wine. In a few minutes, all three were on the ground under the tree, ready for the rats and worms to eat them. They had found Death!

---

1. **the Devil** : in some religions, the opposite of God; the most powerful bad power.
2. **poison** : give a drink that will kill.

The text and **beyond**

1 **Comprehension check**

Answer the following questions. Try to answer from memory; look back at the text only if you really need to.

1   How did the three young men spend most of their time?

2   Why was the bell ringing in the street?

3   What did the three young men decide to do?

4   Who did they meet, and how did they treat him?

5   What did this person tell the young men?

6   What did they find under the tree?

7   Why did the youngest man go to the town?

8   How did the three men die?

2 **The moral**

The Pardoner does not give an explicit moral at the end of the story. In pairs or small groups write a moral in no more than 12 words. Compare your ideas in class and try to agree. In Chaucer's text the Pardoner does, however, say that he uses this story as an example of the message he always gives to people when he speaks in churches. It is on page 111. Is it similar to the moral that you thought of? (It does not matter if it is not; the story can have several morals.)

3 **The Pardoner**

A   When the Pardoner tells us what he does (page 58), does he seem sorry or proud?

B   In *The Canterbury Tales* the story is always suitable for the person telling the story. Why do you think Chaucer gives the Pardoner this story to tell?

4 **Discussion**

1   Who do you think the old man is?

2   What do you think the pile of gold coins represents?

9 5 The Merchant's Tale

FCE

Listen to *The Merchant's Tale*. For questions 1-9, tick (✓) the best answer, A, B or C.

1 The Knight was
 A ☐ rich and handsome.
 B ☐ old but rich.
 C ☐ handsome but old.

2 The Knight's wife was
 A ☐ young and beautiful.
 B ☐ young and rich.
 C ☐ rich and old.

3 May was in love with
 A ☐ January.
 B ☐ Damian.
 C ☐ her servant.

4 January became more jealous of May because
 A ☐ he was blind.
 B ☐ he held her hand.
 C ☐ he knew she loved Damian.

5 May managed to be with Damian by
 A ☐ leaving her husband in the garden.
 B ☐ climbing into a pear tree.
 C ☐ kissing her husband passionately.

6 Who gave January his sight back?
 A ☐ May
 B ☐ Damian
 C ☐ the gods

7 January saw May

    A ☐ fighting Damian in the tree.

    B ☐ kissing Damian in the tree.

    C ☐ talking to the doctor.

8 May told January that

    A ☐ he had made a mistake.

    B ☐ she loved Damian.

    C ☐ she was kissing a young man.

9 What happened to Damian?

    A ☐ He fell out of the tree.

    B ☐ He escaped.

    C ☐ He had pears for supper.

6 Discussion

    1 Why are the two main characters called January and May?

    2 January became physically blind for a while, but is he 'blind' in another way?

    3 Look back to question 3 B above. What do you think the merchant's marriage is like?

7 Men and women

In *The Canterbury Tales* the relationship between men and women is often the theme of a story. You have already read different views of love in Part Two in *The Knight's Tale* and *The Miller's Tale*, and in Part Three you saw the 'marriage' of Chanticleer and Pertelote in *The Nun's Priest's Tale*. How do you feel about the relationship in *The Merchant's Tale*? Choose some of these reactions, and/or add a reaction or reactions of your own, and talk about them.

    A The poor old man! He doesn't deserve a wife like that!

    B The silly old man! He deserves exactly what he gets!

    C The poor young girl! Married to such an old man...

    D The horrible girl! She shouldn't treat her poor husband like that.

    E Your reaction(s): ....

8 Writing

Write a different ending to *The Merchant's Tale* (about 100-120 words). Start from the moment when January gets his sight back. Stick your different endings on a wall, so that the class can see them. How many of them let the woman 'win'? How many let the man 'win'? Are there any happy endings?

9 Traditional tales

Versions of the tales in Part Four can be found in different parts of the world, and are very old. A story of three men who find death in a pile of gold has been told in Asia since the time of the Buddha, 2,500 years ago. Rudyard Kipling included a version of it in *The Second Jungle Book*, and in Europe there have been many versions through the centuries. As far as *The Miller's Tale* is concerned, the unhappy relationship between a young girl and an old man, who is usually seen as comic rather than sad, is very common. Even the moment where a man is tricked by a woman in a pear tree is very common in stories from Europe and Asia. The following story has been told and written in different versions in many languages and cultures. The earliest version seems to come from the Middle East, where in the ninth century the Sufis (very spiritual Muslims) used it for teaching.

Read the story and decide which answer (A, B, C or D) best fits each space. There is an example at the beginning (0).

There was once a rich merchant in Baghdad who was very (**0**) ..A.... of his servant. One morning, as (**1**) ...., the merchant sent his servant to the market to buy food, but not (**2**) .... after he came back, his face completely (**3**) .... He had obviously been (**4**) .... by something. The merchant asked him what the (**5**) .... was. 'I was in the market,' said the servant, 'when I had a strange (**6**) .... It was as if someone was (**7**) .... me. I turned around, and saw a person (**8**) .... at me, with his mouth open wide. He was (**9**) .... black. "Who are you?" I said, terribly afraid. "I am Death," he said. Master, please (**10**) .... me leave Baghdad now, immediately! I can go to my (**11**) .... town, Samarra, and stay with my family. I'll be (**12**) ....

there: Death won't find me there.' The merchant was a very (13) ....
man, and gave his servant his horse so that he could get to Samarra
the evening of the same day. The merchant then went to the market
to (14) .... Death. He found him and said angrily, 'Why did you
frighten my servant this morning?' 'I didn't (15) .... frighten him,'
Death replied. 'It was just that I was surprised to see him here in
Baghdad this morning, because I have an appointment with him
tonight — in Samarra.'

0	**A** fond	**B** affectionate	**C** friendly	**D** kind
1	**A** custom	**B** habit	**C** usual	**D** daily
2	**A** long	**B** much time	**C** long time	**D** very
3	**A** without blood	**B** white	**C** green	**D** without colour
4	**A** awed	**B** afraid	**C** shocked	**D** terrified
5	**A** story	**B** matter	**C** problem	**D** issue
6	**A** sentiment	**B** thought	**C** idea	**D** feeling
7	**A** watching at	**B** staring at	**C** fixing	**D** looking to
8	**A** fingering	**B** showing	**C** indicating	**D** pointing
9	**A** wearing in	**B** dressed in	**C** clothed in	**D** apparelled in
10	**A** let	**B** consent	**C** permit	**D** allow
11	**A** home	**B** family	**C** birth	**D** original
12	**A** careful	**B** certain	**C** secure	**D** safe
13	**A** gentle	**B** friendly	**C** kind	**D** sympathetic
14	**A** search	**B** look for	**C** locate	**D** find out
15	**A** mean to	**B** purpose to	**C** plan for	**D** intend on

10 The moral

Think of a moral for the story in exercise 9. Now compare the story
with *The Pardoner's Tale*. What is similar? What is different?

The City of Canterbury

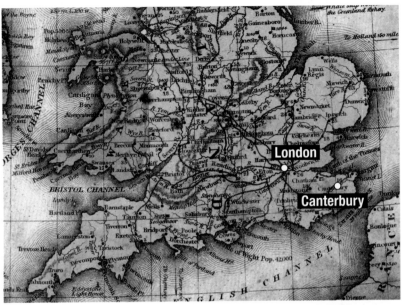

Canterbury is 100 kilometres (62 miles) southeast of London.
The pilgrims probably travelled along Watling Street, a Roman road named
by the Anglo-Saxons, which was ancient even in Chaucer's time.

Canterbury is the city of Becket's murder and of Chaucer's pilgrims.
But it has a far longer history. There was an Iron Age settlement on
the River Stour, Canterbury's small but important river, and Julius
Caesar fought a battle against the Britons near Canterbury. The
Romans built a walled city and named it Durovernum Cantiacorum.
Perhaps the most important event in Canterbury's history took place
in 597, when Saint Augustine arrived from Rome. He met King
Ethelbert, the most powerful ruler in England, and his Christian
wife, Queen Bertha. As a result, Ethelbert and his people became
Christians. Saint Augustine's Abbey was established and

The **Bell Harry** tower of the cathedral.

a cathedral was built. Canterbury became the religious centre of England.

The cathedral is, of course, the most important building in the city. It has developed over many centuries with different architectural [1] styles from Norman (Romanesque) to Victorian (19th century). The main part of the cathedral, however, is Gothic, with a fine central tower called Bell Harry. Canterbury is in a valley [2] so that when the pilgrims came down the hills towards it they had a good view of the cathedral.

There are many buildings from the time of the pilgrims. You can see the Eastbridge Hospital and the Poor Priests' Hospital, where pilgrims could rest. There are two important monasteries on the river. Blackfriars was the home of the Dominicans, who wore black, and Greyfriars was the home of the first Franciscans to come to England. An area just outside the city walls is called Wincheap which means 'wine market'. Pilgrims could buy wine there before they entered the

1. **architectural** : connected with the style of the building.
2. **valley** : a low place between hills.

religious heart of Canterbury, where alcohol was not sold. But today there are as many pubs as churches in the city centre.

The city has many other sights. King's School, just behind the cathedral, is the oldest 'public school' [1] in Britain. The medieval city walls have been rebuilt but one of the city gates,

A fifteenth-century building nowadays used as a pub.

the Westgate with its two towers, remains. Saint Martin's church has the longest history of any church in England. The sixteenth-century 'Weavers' House' is a fine wooden building near the river. However, Canterbury was badly bombed during the Second World War. The cathedral was undamaged but a large part of the historic city was destroyed.

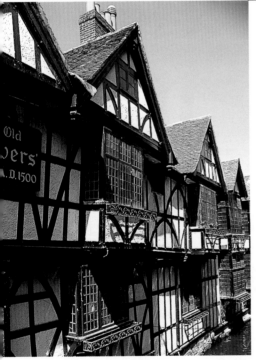

The **Old Weavers' House**.

1. **'public school'** : in Britain, 'public schools' are private schools, not state schools.

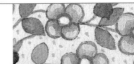

73

You can still easily imagine Chaucer's pilgrims in Canterbury. The Pardoner and the Summoner hurried away to look for victims who would give them money. The Host and the Miller drank together in Wincheap. The Knight went to thank God for his victories in the cathedral while his son, the Squire, walked along the bank of the River Stour with a new girl. The Merchant went to do business in Mercery Lane and the Wife of Bath searched for her sixth husband among the many pilgrims in the crowded city. They had arrived!

Christchurch Gate, the main entrance to the cathedral area.

① Comprehension check

Answer the following questions. Try to answer from memory; look back at the text only if you really need to. Are these sentences true (T) or false (F)? Correct the false ones.

		T	F
1	The Romans fought a battle in Canterbury but did not stay.	☐	☐
2	Saint Augustine succeeded in making the king a Christian.	☐	☐
3	The Cathedral is mainly Norman and Victorian in style.	☐	☐
4	Canterbury is on a hill so that it can be seen from far away.	☐	☐
5	The buildings from Chaucer's time were destroyed by bombs.	☐	☐
6	There are walls around the city.	☐	☐
7	There are two city gates which are still there.	☐	☐
8	The Wife of Bath got married in Canterbury.	☐	☐

T: GRADE 7

② Speaking – village and city life

Bring in a picture or an article about a village or a city in your country that you like. Use it to talk about:

1 the reasons why you like this village or city.
2 its origins and history.
3 its advantages and disadvantages for living in: what you would like/dislike about living in this place.
4 why you prefer it to other villages or cities in your country.

Before you read

① Reading pictures

Look at the picture on page 81. A queen is sitting on a throne. In front of her is a knight with a sword and a group of women. One of the women seems different from the others. Which one? What do you think is her relationship to the knight?

The Wife of Bath's Tale

long time ago, when King Arthur ruled the land, there was a great knight who loved all the pleasures of life. But one day, a lady of the court told the king that the knight had attacked her.

Arthur was very angry and said that the knight must die. 'Cut off his head!' But the Queen and her ladies asked Arthur to give the knight to them for punishment. To please his queen, Arthur agreed.

The Queen sent for the knight. 'I and my ladies have the power to let you live or die,' she said. 'You will live only if you can answer this question: What is it that women most desire? [1] If you cannot tell us at this moment, you may go away for a year and a day to find the answer. But if you return without the answer, remember this: the axe [2] is sharp!'

The knight was very unhappy but he had no choice. He said goodbye to the Queen and rode away.

---

1. **desire** : want very much.
2. **axe** : a sharp instrument, used to cut down trees, or cut off heads!

He travelled through the whole country, from coast to coast, looking for the answer. He knocked on every door. 'What is it that women most desire?' he asked. But he could not find two people who agreed.

'Women want to be rich.'

'No, they want a good reputation.'

'No, they want pleasure.'

'They want fine clothes.'

'They want a life of love with many husbands.'

'Women want to be spoilt and flattered.' [1]

'Women want freedom, with nobody to criticise them.'

'Women want people to say that they can keep a secret.'

That is nonsense, of course. No woman can keep a secret. Do you remember the ancient tale of King Midas? Midas grew a splendid pair of donkey's ears under his long hair. Nobody knew except his wife. Midas loved her and made her promise that she wouldn't tell anyone about his ears. Of course, she promised but, because she was a woman, it was difficult to keep the secret. It wanted to fly out of her mouth.

'I must tell somebody,' she thought. So, she ran down to the lake, her heart on fire. She lay down among the river grasses and whispered [2] the secret to the water. 'My husband has a pair of donkey's ears.' The wind spread the secret through the whole country. We women are all like that.

Well, the knight realised that he would never find the answer. He felt sad and hopeless. The year had finished and this was the day when he had to return to the Queen.

---

1. **flattered** : told nice things about themselves.
2. **whispered** : said very quietly.

As he was riding sadly back to the court through the forest, he suddenly saw twenty-four beautiful women dancing on the green grass. 'Perhaps they know the answer,' he thought. He approached them but, as he did so, they vanished from his sight. It had been a magic vision. Remember that, in the days of King Arthur, there were still fairies [1] in the world.

There was no living thing in the forest except an old woman sitting on the grass where they had danced. She was the ugliest, most horrible creature he had ever seen.

This ugly hag [2] stood up and said, 'Sir Knight, there is no path here. Tell me, what are you looking for? Perhaps I can help. We old people know many things.'

'Old lady, I will die today unless I can answer this question. What is it that women most desire? If you can tell me, I'll pay you well.'

'Give me your hand,' said the hag. 'Promise me that, if I give you the true answer, you will do anything that I ask.'

'I promise,' agreed the knight.

'Then your life is safe. The Queen herself will agree with my answer. The proudest lady that ever wore beautiful clothes will admit that I am right. Let me teach you the answer.' And the old woman whispered in his ear.

When they came to the Queen's court, the knight said, 'I am ready to give my answer.'

The Queen and all her ladies were there. There were single women and wives and many widows, who are the wisest of all. The knight was the only man, surrounded by women. 'Speak!'

---

1. **fairies** : imaginary creatures with magical powers.
2. **hag** : ugly old woman.

said the Queen, who sat like a judge. 'Silence everyone. Listen to the knight.'

The knight spoke loudly so that all the ladies could hear. 'My sweet Queen,' he said, 'women desire to have power over their husbands. This is your greatest desire. Kill me if you like, but this is the true answer.'

There was no woman in the court, not a girl or a wife or a widow, who disagreed with him. 'You may keep your life!' said the Queen.

At that moment, the old hag jumped up and spoke. 'O powerful Queen,' she said, 'before you go, give me justice. I taught the knight how to answer. In return, he said that he would do whatever I asked him. Therefore, before this court, I ask you, Sir Knight, to marry me. I have saved your life. Now do this for me.'

The knight answered unhappily. 'I know that I promised you this. But please change your request. I'll give you everything I have but let my body be mine.'

'No! I'm ugly and old and poor. But I don't want gold or land or luxuries. I want to be your wife and, more than that, I want to be your love!'

'My love? That is impossible.'

But the knight could not escape. He married the hag secretly next day and hid himself for the rest of the day. There was no dancing, no singing or eating and drinking at their wedding.

That night, he lay in bed with her. He turned to and fro [1] like someone with a bad dream, keeping as far away from her as possible.

---

1. **turned to and fro** : turned from side to side continuously.

His old wife lay there, smiling. 'Dear husband, does every one of King Arthur's knights behave like this with his bride? I am your own sweet wife. I have saved your life. I have never done anything bad to you. Why do you behave like this on our first night together? Tell me the problem and I will make it right.'

'Make it right? No, impossible. You are so ugly, so old, and you come from such a low family that I don't want to be near you.'

'Is that all? If you treat me well, I can make this right in three short days. But why do you worry about my family? Don't you know that true gentlewomen and true gentlemen are the ones who do good things. Lords and ladies can become thieves and murderers and cheats. But a poor man or woman can be a true gentleperson if he or she loves God and other human beings.

'You say that I am poor. There is nothing wrong in that. Jesus himself chose to live as a poor man. I think that the poor man is rich, even if he has no shirt. The poor man can always find a song to sing. He is not afraid of thieves. He loves God. He knows that his friends love him for himself and not for his money. It is good to be poor, I think.

'Lastly, you said that I am old and ugly. But you know that all the best writers tell us to respect old people. And if I'm ugly, you needn't be afraid that I will cheat you with another man. But I know what men like. I will give you great pleasure.

'Now, choose one of these two things. You can have me old and ugly until I die. I will be a true wife to you and never upset [1] you as long as I live. Or you can have me young and beautiful. But then men will visit your house while you are away because I am so beautiful. Now choose. Which do you want?'

---

1. **upset** : make someone feel sad, worried or angry.

The knight thought about this for a long time. It made him very unhappy. At last, he spoke.

'My lady and my love, my darling wife, I put myself in your power. Choose yourself. You are wise enough to know which way is the best for you and for me. I don't care what you decide. If you are pleased, then I am also happy.'

'Are you really giving me the power to choose? Will you do as I say?'

'Yes, wife; it is best.'

'Then kiss me. We'll stop being angry with each other. I'll be both things to you. I mean that I'll be young and beautiful but also a true wife. I'll be the best wife that anyone has ever had in the history of the world. If, tomorrow, when the sun is shining, I am not as beautiful as any queen in the east or west, then kill me if you like. Take the curtain from the window. It is morning already, husband. Look at me.'

When the knight looked at her, he saw that she really was young and beautiful. He caught her in his arms and gave her a thousand kisses. She did everything she could to please him.

So they lived in perfect joy. Please God, send all of us women young, strong, handsome husbands who will do anything for our love. And if any men won't give women what they most desire — the power over their husbands — let God strike them dead!

The text and **beyond**

1 Comprehension check

Answer the following questions. Try to answer from memory; look back at the text only if you really need to.

1 On what condition did the Queen allow the knight to live?
2 What happened when the knight asked people his question?
3 What did the knight promise to the old woman in the forest?
4 Were the Queen and her court satisfied with the knight's answer?
5 What did the old woman ask in the Queen's court?
6 What were the knight's three explanations for why he couldn't bear to be near the old woman?
7 What choice did the old woman offer the knight?
8 How does the knight's reply relate to the answer that he gave at the Queen's court?
9 How did the old woman react to the knight's reply?

2 The moral

What moral does the Wife of Bath want to teach us with her story? In pairs or small groups write this moral in no more than 12 words. Compare your ideas in class.

3 Characters

Which character do you prefer, the knight or the woman? Make a list of all the reasons why you prefer one character and all the reasons why you don't like the other character.

4 Feminism

Some people see the Wife of Bath as an early feminist (a person who supports equal rights for women). Find a few sentences and paragraphs in the story that support a feminist interpretation. You do not need to discuss this lot now: in question 7 you will have the chance to talk about it.

11 ⑤ The Wife of Bath

FCE **A** **In the original text, Chaucer gives the Wife of Bath a long 856-line prologue: it is two-thirds as long as her story! Listen to some of it. For questions 1-10, tick (✓) T (True) or F (False).**

		T	F
1	The Wife of Bath was twelve years old when she was first married.	☐	☐
2	She has had six husbands.	☐	☐
3	Her first three husbands controlled her.	☐	☐
4	She became rich because of them.	☐	☐
5	She thinks that money is more important than love.	☐	☐
6	Her fourth husband was more difficult to control.	☐	☐
7	She treated him badly.	☐	☐
8	She gave him an expensive funeral.	☐	☐
9	She is no longer interested in love.	☐	☐
10	She has been a good wife to all her husbands.	☐	☐

11

FCE **B** **Listen again and complete the sentences.**

1 Real .... comes from experience.

2 Everything is for ....

3 Why spend money ....?

4 I've had a .... of love.

5 Although I've lost my ...., I still know how to ....

⑥ Discussion

When Chaucer wrote *The Wife of Bath's Prologue* he used a lot of ideas from anti-feminist writing of the Middle Ages. So, is *The Wife of Bath's Prologue and Tale* feminist or anti-feminist? Choose one of the following interpretations, or make up your own interpretation, and discuss them in class.

A Chaucer lets the Wife of Bath speak for a long time, so he lets her confirm all the worst things about women! She does this all through her prologue, and in her tale, too; for example, when she talks about Midas's wife (page 77). Chaucer does the same thing with the Pardoner (page 58): he lets him condemn himself with his own words!

B Chaucer must think the Wife of Bath is an important character because he gives her such a long prologue. In her story he lets her show us that men only want superficial things in women: physical beauty and youth. In her prologue he lets her speak openly about her life, and with humour. If a man spoke like that people would say he was honest and amusing!

C Your own interpretation: ....

....

FCE **7** **Word formation**

Read the information below about where the story of the ugly old woman comes from. Use the word in capitals at the end of each line to form a word that fits in the space of the same line. There is an example at the beginning (0).

THE 'LOATHLY LADY'

In *The Wife of Bath's Tale*, Chaucer uses the
(**0**) traditional...... folk tale of the 'Loathly Lady' ('loathly'   TRADITION
is an old word meaning ugly). In the (**1**) ....   EARLY
versions of this tale, which are very old and are found in
Celtic (**2**) .... , a woman has been put under a   MYTH
magic spell and has the (**3**) .... of an ugly old   APPEAR
woman. She can only break the spell if she asks a man
for a kiss or even (**4**) .... and he agrees. But   MARRY
first she offers the man the (**5**) ....of having   CHOOSE
her 'fair by day and foul (that is, ugly) by night' or 'fair
by night and foul by day'. Chaucer changes this: she can
be foul and (**6**) .... or fair but not. The knight   FAITH
doesn't choose himself; he leaves the (**7**) ....   DECIDE
to the woman, and this gives the Wife of Bath a
feminist moral for her story.
In Celtic and medieval 'Loathly Lady' tales, the woman
is an (**8**) .... ; she has to live far away from   OUTSIDE
society, on her own. But, in spite of her (**9**) ....,   UGLY
people come often looking for her: she is the only
person with some special (**10**) .... that is   KNOW
important for the hero or for society.

8 Traditional tales

A   In the well-known story *Beauty and the Beast* the 'Beast', an ugly monster, changes into a handsome prince when a young woman, 'Beauty', says she will marry him and so breaks the spell. Beauty says she will marry the Beast because she really has fallen in love with him: this is an important difference from *The Wife of Bath's Tale*. Do you know this story?

B   Do you know any stories from your culture, or other cultures, where women and/or men are transformed (that is, changed) from being old and/or ugly — or even an animal — into being young and beautiful/handsome? How are they similar to or different from *The Wife of Bath's Tale*? How are men and women treated in these stories?

9 Vocabulary – adjectives and nouns

A   Change these adjectives into nouns. The first one has been done for you.

1	affectionate: *affection*	7	beautiful: ....
2	comfortable:	8	famous: ....
3	free:	9	happy: ....
4	healthy:	10	independent: ....
5	luxurious:	11	respectful: ....
6	successful:	12	wealthy: ....

B   Add to the list two or three other similar adjectives and nouns — that is, about what people might want. Share your ideas in class.

C   Now write sentences about what different people want, using either adjectives or nouns. Think of many different people.

For example: *Most people want their partners to be affectionate.*

or   *Most people want affection from their partners.*
            More than anything, I want to be free.

or   *More than anything, I want freedom.*

D   Is it possible to answer these questions?

- What is it that women most desire?
- What is it that men most desire?

🔟 Writing
Write a short story (minimum 150 words, maximum — your choice) about a transformation. There must be a 'person A' and a 'person B'. Think about these questions, but you can add your own ideas:

- Who ('person A') is under a spell, and why? What does he/she/it look like now?
- Who ('person B') arrives to break this spell?
- Why does 'person B' arrive?
- Why does 'person B' help 'person A'? For love? For duty? Because it is necessary at that moment? Because he/she is tricked? ...
- What happens next?
- What is the ending like? Happy? Sad? Tragic? Comic? Mysterious? Open? ...
- Is there a moral?

If you like, you can update a traditional story. For example, the fairy story Cinderella, where the heroine is transformed, was 'transformed' into the Hollywood film *Pretty Woman* (1990).

Before you read

1 Reading pictures
Look at the picture on page 91. What is the woman looking at? What do you think that she is thinking? Write down her thoughts in one sentence. Compare your sentences in class.

PART SIX

The Franklin's Tale

'I am a simple man,' said the Franklin. 'I haven't read many books. But I will tell my story simply and clearly.

'A long time ago, in Brittany, [1] there was a knight who loved a lady. She was one of the most beautiful women under the sun and came from a noble family. He was afraid to speak to her but at last he asked her to marry him.

She knew how much he loved her and decided to accept him as her husband and her lord. In return, he promised that he would never use his power against her but would always do what she wanted. He would never forget that he was her lover as well as her husband.

'Sir,' she said, 'you have given me everything I want from marriage — love and independence. I will be your true wife until I die. My heart is yours.'

This is the best kind of marriage. Love will not be limited by

1. **Brittany** : a region of north-west France.

power. When one person tries to control the other, the God of Love beats his wings and, farewell, he is gone! Women want to be free, not to be servants. And men are the same.

So the lady took the knight as her servant in love and her lord in marriage. If you are not married, you can't imagine the happiness that a wife and husband can enjoy.

Soon, however, the knight, whose name was Arveragus, had to go to England to fight. He stayed there for two years. His wife, whose name was Dorigen, loved her husband as much as she loved her own life. While he was away, she cried and sighed [1] and lost her appetite. She could not sleep and paid no attention to the world. Arveragus sent her letters, telling her how much he loved her. At last, she began to recover. She drove away her dark fantasy.

Her castle was on the coast, next to the sea. Dorigen often walked with her friends along the clifftop [2] but, when she saw the ships on the sea, she began to cry. 'If one of these ships brought home my lord, then my heart would be happy.'

There were terrible black rocks in the sea. Her heart trembled with fear. 'God, why did you make these black rocks and put them here in the sea? They are no good for anything. They destroy ships. Thousands of men have died at sea. It kills my heart to look at them.'

One morning in May, her friends had a party for her. They wanted to make her happy. They went to a garden full of flowers with their bright colours and sweet perfumes; a little paradise. After dinner, they began to dance and sing. But Dorigen stayed

---

1. **sighed** : breathed deeply and sadly.
2. **clifftop** : the top of a high hill above the sea.

alone. She could not be happy without Arveragus.

At this party, there was one of her neighbours, a young squire named Aurelius. He was as bright and handsome as May itself. He was young, strong, honest, rich and wise; a perfect lover. He had loved Dorigen secretly for two years but had never told her. He had written many songs and poems about a beautiful lady that he loved hopelessly, but she herself had no idea that she was the lady!

Aurelius decided that the time had come to open his heart.

'Madam, my heart is breaking. You can kill me or save my life with one word. I lie here at your feet. Give me your sweet love or I will die.'

'What are you saying?' said Dorigen. 'I will never be an untrue wife. Take this as my final answer.' But, after this, she added as a joke, 'Aurelius, I would give you my love if you could remove the black rocks from the sea. If you can do that, I'll love you more than any other man!'

'Is there no other way to win your love?'

'No, by God. Forget this stupid idea. Why do you want another man's wife?'

'Madam,' said Aurelius, 'it is impossible to remove the rocks. So, I will die for your love.' With these words, he left her. At his house, he shivered with cold. His heart was ice. He got down on his knees and spoke to the gods.

'Apollo, god of the sun, help me. Your sister, the goddess of the moon, has power over the seas and rivers. Ask her to make a great flood [1] which covers the black rocks. Then I can go to my

---

1. **flood** : when the water rises and covers the land.

92

lady and say, Look! I have won your love!' With those words, Aurelius fell on the floor. Luckily, his brother found him and carried him to bed.

Now it is time for me to tell you about Arveragus. He came back from the wars after he had won many battles. Dorigen, you are so happy now! Your husband is in your arms! He loves you better than his own life and never imagines that another man has spoken to you about love.

Aurelius was lovesick for two years. He stayed in bed and told no-one about his desire for Dorigen except his brother. His brother was very worried. 'How can I help Aurelius?' he asked himself. 'I remember that when I was in the city of Orléans, [1] I saw a secret book. There are students of magic who can make a river flow inside a house or a lion appear at a dance. They can make people see a castle suddenly appear and then, when they wish, it disappears again.'

So his brother told Aurelius about the book. Aurelius immediately decided to go to Orléans with him. As they came near the city, a young man met him. 'I know why you are here,' he said. 'I am the magician who can help you.' This man took the brothers to his house and showed them fantastic things. Knights fought a great battle in front of their eyes. Then Aurelius saw Dorigen dancing and went to join her. The magician clapped his hands. Everything disappeared!

The magician promised to make all the black rocks disappear from the coast of Brittany. 'But you must pay me a thousand pounds. Nothing less.'

---

1. **Orléans** : a city in central France.

Aurelius laughed. 'I would give you the round world if you could help me win the love of Dorigen. I promise to pay you.'

Next day, the brothers and the magician rode back to the coast. It was December, the beginning of winter when all the green had disappeared from the world. There was frost [1] and rain and snow. 'Please act quickly,' begged [2] Aurelius. 'If I have to wait longer, I will kill myself for love.'

The magician was sorry for him and worked day and night. He took out his magic books and chose the best time for his trick. The moon and stars were in the right place in the sky. Then, by magic, the rocks became invisible. No one could see them.

Aurelius went to the cliff and looked. Then he fell at the magician's feet. 'Thank you, my lord, and thank you, Lady Venus.' [3] He went quickly to find Dorigen.

'My true lady,' he began, 'you almost killed me when you did not give me your love. But now, remember your promise and do not murder me. I have done what you wanted. The black rocks have gone. Go and look. Then, if you decide to be true to your promise, come to me at the garden! We will be lovers there!'

Dorigen lost all the colour from her face. 'I have been tricked! I never imagined that it would be possible to remove the rocks.' She went home and cried for two days without stopping. Arveragus was in another town, so she had no one to help her. 'I must choose between breaking my promise to Aurelius or being

1. **frost** : ice on the ground.
2. **begged** : asked very much.
3. **Venus** : classical goddess of love.

an untrue wife. There is only one solution. Many famous women in history have killed themselves to escape from men who tried to take their love. I will be one of them.'

On the third day, however, Arveragus came home. 'Why are you crying, my darling wife?' he asked her.

She told him everything. Arveragus was not angry but spoke softly to her. 'My dear wife, I cannot ask you to break your promise. My love for you tells me that you must be true. Truth is the highest thing in a person's life!' Then he suddenly began to cry. 'But never speak to anyone about this thing after you have done it. Now, get ready to go to Aurelius. Be happy. No one must see what is happening.'

Perhaps you think that he was stupid to put his wife in such danger. But listen to the end of my story. Then decide.

Dorigen met Aurelius in the street as she was going to the garden to keep her promise. 'Where are you going?' he asked, his face bright and happy.

She told him everything.

Aurelius was shocked. He realised how much Arveragus loved Dorigen. He decided it was better to forget his love than to make her love him against her will.

'Madam, tell your lord, Arveragus, that I understand his love for you. I will not come between his love and you. I agree to forget all your promises. Madam, you are the best and truest wife I have ever known. Your husband has been generous and I will be generous also.'

Dorigen went down on her knees and thanked him. Then she returned to Arveragus and told him what had happened. They were happy for the rest of their lives and lived like a king and queen of love.

Aurelius realised that he had lost everything. 'I must pay the magician a thousand pounds. I must sell my house and all my land. But I must keep my promise.'

Sadly, he went to the magician. 'I can pay you five hundred pounds,' he said. 'Please, give me time to pay the rest.'

'Didn't I keep my promise to you?' asked the magician.

'Yes, you did,' replied Aurelius.

'And didn't you enjoy the love of your lady because of my magic?'

'No... No...'

'Tell me the reason if you can.'

'She wanted to kill herself. But her husband loved her so much that he wanted her to be true to her promise. When I heard this, I sent her back to him.'

'My dear friend, you have all done well. He is a knight and he was generous. You are a squire and you were generous. I am a philosopher and I will be generous. I don't want any money for all my work. So now, goodbye!'

The Franklin turned to the other pilgrims. 'My lords, who was the best, most generous gentleman? What do you think?'

The text and **beyond**

1 Comprehension check

Answer the following questions. Try to answer from memory; look back at the text only if you really need to.

1 Which happened first: did Arveragus ask Dorigen to marry him, or did Dorigen ask Arveragus to marry her?

2 What happened soon after they got married?

3 Dorigen was very sad and worried. She saw some things in the sea which seemed to represent all her sadness and worries: what were they?

4 Who had been secretly in love with Dorigen, and for how long?

5 What did Dorigen ask Aurelius to do? Was she serious?

6 What did the magician from Orléans agree to do for Aurelius? Was he able to do it?

7 After Aurelius reminded Dorigen of her promise, what was the first thing she thought of doing?

8 What did Arveragus tell Dorigen to do?

9 How did Aurelius behave to Dorigen, and why?

10 How did the magician behave to Aurelius, and why?

2 Questions of love

In medieval France, an entertainment for women at royal courts was to debate 'questions of love'. Writers then started putting these kinds of questions in stories, as can be seen in *The Canterbury Tales*. The Queen's question in *The Wife of Bath's Tale* is an example, and so is the question the old lady asks the knight (bottom of page 82). Another is in the original version of *The Knight's Tale*, where Chaucer asks 'Which lover is in the worse position: Palamon who is in prison but who can see Emily every day through the bars, or Arcite who is free but can't see or speak to her? (middle of page 30)

The question at the end of the Franklin's story, therefore, was usual in literature in the Middle Ages. But it is still interesting!

Work in pairs. Which of the sentences below (1-9) could apply to the male characters? Put the numbers against each character's name, and say if you think they are positive or neutral comments. Say if you do not agree with the comments, and try to add other comments against each character's name. Then debate which man behaved in the best way.

Arveragus ....

Aurelius ....

The magician ....

1 He is prepared to be terribly hurt so that Dorigen can keep her promise.

2 He has a contract about services and money, not morality. He does what he was asked to do, so it is generous not to insist on payment.

3 He is honest about his love for Dorigen, but does not pressure her, as many men do (for example, other men in stories from *The Canterbury Tales*).

4 His sacrifice is just a question of money. He doesn't give up anything very important.

5 He gives up what he desires the most — but he has no real legal or moral right to have what he desires.

6 He is very professional, and works even harder because he has personal feelings towards the man he has a contract with.

7 He treats Dorigen as an equal, with respect.

8 He allows Dorigen not to keep her promise, allowing her to remain faithful to her husband.

9 Perhaps he has no choice, because the only other solution that Dorigen considers is suicide.

In a version of this tale by the Italian writer Boccaccio, one of the women who has listened to the story decides which man behaves most generously. You can see her decision on page 111. Is it the same as yours?

3 Discussion

What do you think of the character of Dorigen? Write some positive, neutral or even negative comments about her. Then debate whether she deserves to be above or below the character you chose in first position in question 2 above.

4 The pains of love

In medieval love poetry the unsatisfied (usually male) lover experiences the 'pains of love'. This happens in the 'courtly love' tradition (see exercise 7, page 40). When Arcite in *The Knight's Tale* goes back to Thebes, Chaucer describes him like this:

'Without sleep, food and drink, Arcite became as thin and dry as a stick. His eyes became hollow and his face as white as ashes. He was always alone, and all night he complained about his suffering. At the sound of music or singing he started crying. He changed so much that people didn't recognise him. It seemed to everyone that he was not just in love but suffering from a mania...'

Here are the symptoms of unsatisfied love that men usually experience in medieval poetry.

> staying alone   not sleeping   feeling depressed
> praying for death   having no interest in doing anything
> going mad   dressing carelessly   staying in bed for long periods
> having no appetite   having a changed physical appearance
> crying at the sound of music

1   Which of them can you see in *The Franklin's Tale*?

2   In pairs or small groups, decide which of the symptoms above seem most realistic and which seem least realistic.

3   Now find as many of the symptoms as you can in songs (pop, rock, etc.). Quote the lines from the songs if you can.

5 The book against women

You will hear some more from *The Wife of Bath's Prologue*. She is telling the story of her fifth and last husband. As you listen, answer the questions. Listen again if necessary.

1   What was the difference in age between the Wife of Bath and her last husband?

2   Where did they first meet?

3   Was his name Jenkin or Jankin or Junkin?

4 What did she say to him while they were walking?
5 How soon after the end of her fourth marriage did she marry again?
6 What was the book like?
7 What kind of stories were in the book?
8 How many pages did she tear out of the book?
9 Why is the Wife of Bath deaf (unable to hear) in her left ear?
10 Why was he worried?
11 What did he promise?
12 What happened to the book?

6 A perfect marriage

Some critics think that four of *The Canterbury Tales* form a 'marriage group', because they all present different ideas about marriage. In the first in the group, *The Wife of Bath's Tale*, the Wife says that wives should have power over their husbands. The second, told by the Oxford Cleric, is about an obedient wife, Griselda, whose husband cruelly tests her faithfulness. The third, *The Merchant's Tale*, gives a humorous but cruel picture of marriage. Many people think that the fourth and last tale, *The Franklin's Tale*, shows us the ideal marriage, based on equality and freedom (see the top of page 90). Do you think that Arveragus and Dorigen have complete equality in their marriage? Why, or why not?

7 Rash promises

If something is 'rash', you do it too quickly, without thinking about the effects of your action. If you make a 'rash promise' you don't think about what might happen later. Perhaps you don't even think you will need to keep your promise. 'Rash promises' are common elements in stories from different cultures; they are used to develop the plot dramatically. An example from the Bible is when King Herod likes the dancing of Salomé so much that he promises her whatever she wants. When she asks for the head of John the Baptist on a dish he has to give it to her, even though he doesn't want to. In *The Wife of Bath's Tale*, the young knight makes a rash promise to the old woman. He doesn't have much choice when he makes his promise, but there is a happy ending. In *The Franklin's Tale*, Dorigen rashly promises to give herself to Aurelius, but only because Aurelius's task seems impossible. Besides, her real reason for asking Aurelius to remove the rocks is because she wants her husband to come home safely. The story below comes from the collection of fairy tales made by the Grimm brothers in Germany in 1812-15. It involves a rash promise and also a transformation (see exercise 9, page 87).

FCE   Read the story and think of the word which best fits each space. Use only one word in each space. There is an example at the beginning (0).

One morning a princess dropped her favourite thing, a golden ball, and it went (**0**) ..into............. a deep pool. 'If only I could get my ball again, I (**1**) .... give everything I have,' she said. A frog put his head (**2**) .... of the water and said 'I don't want your jewels, (**3**) .... if you let me live with you and sleep on your bed, I (**4**) .... get your ball.' 'This horrible frog can never get to the palace,' thought the princess, 'but he (**5**) .... be able to get my ball.' So she said, 'Well, if you get my ball, I'll do (**6**) .... you ask.' The frog dived under the water, came (**7**) .... with the ball in his mouth, and put it by the edge of the pool. The princess picked it up happily and ran (**8**) .... to the palace.

That evening there was a gentle knock (**9**) .... the door of the royal dining room. The princess opened the door and, frightened, quickly closed it (**10**) .... 'What's the matter?' asked the king, her father. 'There's a horrible frog outside,' said the princess, and explained what (**11**) ....happened. 'You have (**12**) .... a promise, so you must keep it,' said the king. '(**13**) .... him in.' The frog hopped into the room, ate (**14**) .... the princess's plate and asked to be taken to her bedroom. Reluctantly, the princess put him on her pillow. In the morning he jumped (**15**) .... and hopped out of the palace. 'Now I'm free!' thought the princess.

But the (**16**) .... evening the same thing happened, and the third. But the following morning the princess saw a handsome prince standing (**17**) .... her bed. He told her he had (**18**) .... put under a cruel spell, and that he had had to wait (**19**) .... a princess would let him sleep on her bed for three nights. 'You (**20**) .... broken the spell!' said the prince, 'Now, my love, marry me!'

8 Writing

Write a short story (minimum 150 words, maximum — your choice) about a rash promise. It could be a story like one of those in *The Canterbury Tales*, or a fairy story, or a story about a rash promise that you yourself have made (or nearly made!).

9 Chaucer's language – Middle English

The language used in England before the Norman Conquest of 1066 is called 'Old English'. It was a Germanic language, and is sometimes called Anglo-Saxon. The language used from soon after the Norman Conquest till 1500 is called 'Middle English'. In this period (1100-1500) English became grammatically simpler, and used structures and a lot of vocabulary from French, the language of the Normans. The period of 'Modern English' starts from 1500, and continues till now.

Below are some famous lines in Chaucer's original Middle English. They are followed by a rough modern translation. Can you fill in the words missing in the translation? Do you recognise any of the words in Middle English?

From *The Prologue*:

Whan that Aprill with his shoures sote

The droghte of March hath perced to the roote...

Than longen folk to goon on pilgrimages.

When (1) .... with its sweet showers replaces the dry period of (2) ...., then people want to (3) .... on pilgrimages.

From *The Franklin's Tale*:

Love wol nat been constreyned by maistrye.

Whan maistrie comth, the God of Love anon

Beteth his wynges, and farewel, he is gon!

Love will (4) .... be limited by power; when power enters a marriage, the god of love soon beats his (5) .... and — goodbye! — he goes!

The Canterbury Tales

1

Chaucer wrote *The Canterbury Tales* more than six hundred years ago but they are still popular. Why? First of all, because they give a wonderful picture of society in the fourteenth century. Chaucer includes all types of people in his book. There are corrupt [1] church officials. There are people from the higher classes such as the Knight and the Prioress. There are common people such as the Miller and the Host. There are bad characters such as the Pardoner and good characters such as the Parson. Chaucer deals with the important topics of his time. *The Pardoner's Tale* is about the Black Death. *The Wife of Bath's Tale* and *The Franklin's Tale* are about marriage. Religion and war and magic are all included in the world which Chaucer creates.

2

Also, *The Canterbury Tales* are an important part of the development of literature in England. When Chaucer was born, French and Latin were the most powerful languages. Latin was used in the Church and French was the language of the royal court. English, although it was used every day by the majority of the people, was a second-class language. Things changed during Chaucer's lifetime. John Wyclif translated the Bible into English for the first time. And Chaucer himself, encouraged by the example of Italian writers such as Dante, decided to make the everyday English of south-east England and London the language of literature.

1. **corrupt** : dishonest.

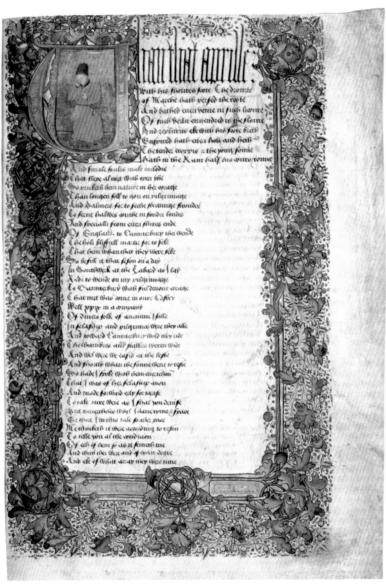

The beginning of the **Prologue**, from a mid-fifteenth-century manuscript of *The Canterbury Tales*.

3

The Canterbury Tales deal with topics and emotions which still interest us today. Through his stories, Chaucer discusses the 'war' between men and women. The Wife of Bath seems to think that women should have the power in a relationship. But the Franklin suggests that both the man and the woman should have freedom and power. Death and greed are themes of *The Pardoner's Tale.* Many characters feel the power of love. Palamon thinks of Emily during his years in prison, Aurelius is sick for two years in his bed, Dorigen can think of nothing except the black rocks which might kill her husband.

4

Chaucer died before he could complete *The Canterbury Tales.* His pilgrims never reached Canterbury. The Romans built a great walled city there. St Augustine brought Christianity to England there. Thomas Becket was murdered there. Chaucer wrote one of the great books of world literature about the journey there. Hundreds of thousands of pilgrims and tourists have travelled there. Canterbury is waiting for you.

1 Comprehension check

Choose from the list A-E the sentence which best summarises each part (1-4) of the text. There is one extra sentence which you do not need to use.

A ☐ A wide range of themes
B ☐ An interesting city
C ☐ Dante's and Boccaccio's influence
D ☐ An insight into Chaucer's times
E ☐ An innovative use of language

Emily being watched by Palamon and Arcite,
from a **French illuminated manuscript**

2 Reading pictures

There are four pairs of pictures below for four of the stories, but for the fifth story there is a picture missing. Which is the story that has a picture missing? Now say what is happening in each picture.

CE ❶ The following questions are about all the stories. For questions 1-8, tick (✓) the answer A, B, C or D which you think fits best according to the text. Try to do this from memory!

1 Chaucer met the pilgrims
   A ☐ in Canterbury.
   B ☐ at the tomb of Thomas Becket.
   C ☐ in London.
   D ☐ in the forest.

2 How many people were in the group when they left early in the morning?
   A ☐ 29
   B ☐ 30
   C ☐ 31
   D ☐ 32

3 Theseus decides to let Arcite and Palamon live because
   A ☐ they are no longer the enemies of Athens.
   B ☐ what they have done, they have done for love.
   C ☐ he is in love with Emily.
   D ☐ he wants to watch them fight.

4 Chanticleer's dream
   A ☐ is a result of eating too much.
   B ☐ comes true.
   C ☐ makes him laugh.
   D ☐ is about a coward.

5 The fox releases Chanticleer from his mouth because
   A ☐ Chanticleer tricks him.
   B ☐ Chanticleer is too heavy.
   C ☐ he wants Chanticleer to sing.
   D ☐ Chanticleer is stupid.

6 What do the three young men ultimately find under the tree?
   A ☐ a pile of gold
   B ☐ the old man
   C ☐ Death
   D ☐ poison

7 The knight of King Arthur's court tells his wife that he wants her

A ☐ to be young and beautiful.

B ☐ to be old, ugly and true.

C ☐ to decide for herself.

D ☐ to go away.

8 Dorigen promises Aurelius her love if

A ☐ he removes the black rocks from the sea.

B ☐ he writes her songs and poems.

C ☐ he dies for her.

D ☐ Arveragus returns home safely.

2 **Answer the following questions.**

1 According to Chaucer, who were the two bad people of the group and why were they bad?

2 In *The Knight's Tale* why do Arcite and Palamon fight? Who wins in the end?

3 How does Chanticleer manage to escape from the fox in the *Nun's Priest's Tale*?

4 Why do the three young men in *The Pardoner's Tale* die?

5 In *The Wife of Bath's Tale* what is women's greatest desire?

6 Why does Aurelius release Dorigen from her obligation to him in *The Franklin's Tale*?

3 **The tales contain many different themes. Below is a list of the most important ones in the stories you have read. Match them to the correct tales. You can use a theme more than once.**

generosity   greed   dreams   love   friendship   pride
misogyny¹   bravery   chivalry   deception   role of fate   death
relationship between husband and wife   magic

1 *The Knight's Tale*   ....

2 *The Nun's Priest's Tale*   ....

3 *The Pardoner's Tale*   ....

4 *The Wife of Bath's Tale*   ....

5 *The Franklin's Tale*   ....

1 **misogyny** : hating women.

110

4 Writing

Which tale did you enjoy the most? Write a short composition (about 200-250 words) explaining your choice.

Key to Exit Test

1 1C 2B 3B 4B 5A 6C 7C 8A

2 **1** The Summoner and the Pardoner. The Summoner because he used his power to cheat poor people. The Pardoner because he, too, used his religious powers to cheat people.

3 Because he tricks the fox by flattering him and telling him to talk. In this way the fox releases Chanticleer from his jaws and he escapes.

4 They are unpleasant people, but they find death because they are greedy.

5 Women's greatest desire is to have power over their husbands.

6 Because he realises how much she loves her husband, and because he wants to behave generously as Dorigen's husband did.

3 **1** *The Knight's Tale*: love, friendship, bravery, role of fate.

2 *The Nun's Priest's Tale*: dreams, love, pride, deception, relationship between husband and wife.

3 *The Pardoner's Tale*: greed, friendship, deception, death.

4 *The Wife of Bath's Tale*: generosity, love, misogyny, relationship between husband and wife.

5 *The Franklin's Tale*: generosity, love, chivalry, relationship between husband and wife, magic.

Page 66 Exercise 2

Open answer. The Pardoner uses a Latin phrase: Radix malorum est cupiditas; the love of money is the root of evil (root = cause, origin).

Page 99 Exercise 2

In Boccaccio's version of this tale (the *Filocolo*), a woman called Fiammetta decides that the husband is the most generous, because he offers to sacrifice his honour.

2 They fight because they both love the same woman — Emily. In the end Arcite wins the battle but is then thrown from his horse and dies, so Palamon wins Emily's love in the end.

This reader uses the **EXPANSIVE READING** approach, where the text becomes a springboard to improve language skills and to explore historical background, cultural connections and other topics suggested by the text.

The new structures introduced in this step of our READING & TRAINING series are listed below. Naturally, structures from lower steps are included too. For a complete list of structures used over all the six steps, see *The Black Cat Guide to Graded Readers*, which is also downloadable at no cost from our website, www.blackcat-cideb.com or www.cideb.it.

The vocabulary used at each step is carefully checked against vocabulary lists used for internationally recognised examinations.

Step Four B2.1

All the structures used in the previous levels, plus the following:

Verb tenses
Present Perfect Simple: *the first / second* etc. *time that ...*
Present Perfect Continuous: unfinished past with *for* or *since* (duration form)

Verb forms and patterns
Passive forms: Present Perfect Simple
Reported speech introduced by precise reporting verbs (e.g. *suggest, promise, apologise*)

Modal verbs
Be / get used to + *-ing*: habit formation
Had better: duty and warning

Types of clause
3rd Conditional: *if* + Past Perfect, *would(n't) have*
Conditionals with *may / might*
Non-defining relative clauses with: *which, whose*
Clauses of concession: *even though*; *in spite of, despite*

Available at Step Four: